And Don't Call Us
... LADIES!

PAMELA NELSON & KIMBERLY RICOTTA

Copyright © 2016 ADCUL LLC

All rights reserved, including the right to reproduce this book or portions thereof in any form whatsoever without the express written permission of ADCUL LLC.

Contact: publishers@rojeecrumbefilms.com

www.rojeecrumbefilms.com

ISBN 978-0-9673590-2-1

Illustrations: Vincent Merino

For our families and friends,
with love and gratitude.
And, most especially, for our Sherpas.

What I wanted to do was to paint sunlight on the side of a house.

   — *Edward Hopper*

FOREWORD

When someone recently asked us why, after twenty years, we decided to write *And Don't Call Us ... Ladies!*, our reply was simple. Because we think it's a good story, ready for the picking after twenty years on the vine. But what kind of story is it? A cautionary tale? An inspirational one? Entertainment, pure and simple? All three, we hope. But let the reader decide. At the end of the day, we like to think it's a celebration of the fact that we're all human and have the right, if not the personal obligation, to bounce back from adversity and keep on heading for the moon, or at least the corner grocery store.

―――

Though Pam is the primary narrator of this story, both Pam and Kim worked in tandem to decide what and how much to include in this book. In all other ways as well this has been a collaborative project, made possible in no small way by Kim's having tenaciously held onto the production files, including her copious twenty-year-old notes, budgets, invoices, memos, faxes, phone logs and conversations, and other documentation, all of which proved invaluable in refreshing and corroborating – and sometimes refuting – our imperfect memories. That being said, while we've done our best to accurately reconstruct events, there may still be some inconsistencies in the timeline, and some other minor discrepancies.

―――

The people and situations portrayed in this story are real. However, some of the names and identifying elements have been changed.

PRELUDE

THE VIPER - Rock Bottom in D Minor

I thought a stick was a snake. Until it bit me, and then I knew.
— **Jarod Kintz**, *Whenever You're Gone, I'm Here For You*

THE VIPER
Rock Bottom in D Minor

Early December 1996 – *Candi (our "new" investor and Executive Producer) is in default, but her myriad money connections keep filing in – in person, or on the phone. We've yet to meet a credible contact, yet we have no choice but to check them all out.*

The Viper walked in and set his briefcase on the table. That wasn't his real name – just the name we had given him as a result of Candi telling us, ad infinitum, that he drove a Viper.

"This is Lamarr," Candi said as she proudly escorted him into the room. "Did I tell you he drives a Viper?"

"How are you?" I asked, shaking the Viper's sweaty hand. Well, at least, it wouldn't be quite so sweaty when Kim took a turn at it. "Have a seat."

The Viper stumbled over a chair, fell into it, and then proceeded to hang off one side of it, such that his fingers literally rested on the floor. We nicknamed him the Viper, but we could just as easily have dubbed him *Sideways Man*. His hair was long and greasy and he wore sunglasses that he never took off. He could also have been *the Dude's*[1] skinny, but deeply unattractive, evil twin. Or Rasputin on Valium.

Trying to find his eyes beneath the dark lenses (but failing), I cut to the chase. "So, Candi says you're interested in our film."

"Yeppugs. Swinginthing potenchki messaloni roofala achum." Can't swear those were the exact words he muttered, but I think I'm pretty close. In fact, neither Kim, nor I, was able to make out a word he was saying. You could ask the guy to speak up – which we did – but the gibberish only got louder, and our lack of comprehension more offensive to him. "SWINGINTHING POTENCHKI FUCKINA MESSALONI ROOFALA. ACHUM!"

Indeed.

If only the Viper had been speaking a foreign language, we could have worked our way toward some sort of linguistic middle ground. Unfortunately, this was drug-speak, and neither Kim nor I had majored in it.

Candi had though, and that was a relief. "Did I tell you he drives a Viper?" she beamed.

The Viper continued his incomprehensible sales pitch, injecting dollar signs into the equation for good measure. "Swinginthing million fuckina messaloni… four million potenchki achum fuckina roofala." That said, he opened his briefcase and pulled out shiny, four-color brochures that outlined his wealth of precious gems. Laying them on the table in front of us, he waited for our reaction.

Clearly, he was due for a fix.

Suddenly, I felt my spine lengthen and righteous indignation well up like bile from a churning gallbladder.

"Kim," I said as calmly as possible, "can I see you in the hallway for a minute?"

The door safely shut behind us, I hit the ceiling pretty hard, though my anger, as Kim well knew, wasn't directed at her, but at those who remained in the room. "I want that guy the fuck out of here *now!*"

The "F" word? As a mother of four children who still lived at home, I usually kept that one at bay, lest it should slip out at an inopportune moment. Kim was impressed. Well, maybe not impressed, but pretty sure I had flipped out.

"I'll go get Candi," she said.

Candi joined us in the hallway where I told her as plainly as I knew how, "I want that guy out of here *now!*" No "F word" this time, but in the spirit of repressed expletives, my hands were shaking. In fact, my whole body was shaking.

Had our film really come to THIS?

I felt sick. Kim felt sick. Years of pounding the pavement to raise development money, achieving the seemingly impossible by securing a bona fide production investor, polishing the script (over and over again), all the many wonderful people attached depending on us... reduced to this moment in time. It was as if the Viper had come to us as the emissary of hell, on a mission to convey to us just how screwed we really were.

The least we could do was have Candi "shoo" the messenger.

Candi nodded. She dutifully asked the Viper to disappear, which he did – but not without leaving the contents of his briefcase behind. Perhaps, thought he, once we took the time to thoroughly examine his net worth in precious gems, we would come running back to him, drug-speak interpreter in tow.

That certainly wasn't going to happen. But here's one thing that was going to happen. We were both going to run straight to our respective homes and take a long, soul-cleansing shower.

The moral of the story hardly needs saying, but what the heck – say it with me:

You can't judge a man by his viper. Or by his gems, for that matter.

That said, when the emissary of hell comes knocking, you can always ask him to go back to hell.

Kim and I had hit rock bottom. Yet, somehow, we had to find the courage to keep on going, to keep on hoping, to keep on facing each day no matter what the long-range forecast – despite the fact that a hurricane of movie madness was building momentum, making its way directly toward us.

1 – The main character from the Coen Brothers' movie, *The Big Lebowski*.

ACT ONE

THE INTERSECTION OF BRAVE & FOOLHARDY - Two Screenwriters on a Mission

LAUNDRY ROOOM OPERATIONS - Is That my Uncle Flying Past the Window?

VELVET- Driving Through Roswell, NM with an Alien in the Passenger Seat

SHOE IN THE ROAD - The Office on Squirrel Street

THE FACE OF A BRIEFCASE - What More Could Two Girls Ask For?

NO TIME FOR THE GIGGLES – A Gallic Dinner with our Director

FINDING THE FINDER - How a Painter's Eavesdropping Paid Off

GOING HOWARD-KEELING - Time-Traveling in a Gold-Plated Lexus

CASTING & CRUMPETS - Does Life Get Any Sweeter Than This?

SINGIN' IN THE RAIN WE'RE NOT – Air Cuts and the Fight over Kim's Umbrella

PING-PONG, ANYONE? - Hindsight Won't Get You a Cup of Coffee

MONEY, MONEY, MONEY - Scrambling to Keep Pace

OUR KARMA HAS A FACE - Does Money Wear a Tight Skirt?

THINGS GET UGLY - New Outfits and an Empty Bank Account

A BUCKET OF PAIN – The Case of the Fleeing Intern

BATHTUB BLUES – A Heart for Any Fate

A GRINDING HALT – The Long Bridge to Nowhere

LAST-DITCH EFFORTS – Marty's Leg to Stand On

THE LONGEST DAY – The Day of the Frozen Parakeets

THE INTERSECTION OF BRAVE & FOOLHARDY
Two Screenwriters on a Mission

March 1993 – *Kim and I are never formally introduced, but we manage to find each other in the crowd. We talk film. We laugh. We hit it off. We don't realize it yet, but's we're standing on a centrifuge. Before we know it, our world is going to start spinning and the bottom will drop out from under our feet. We've barely said hello, but it's the beginning of a wild and crazy ride.*

Kim stands at about 4' 11" and, in the spring of 1993, sported a fashionable expanse of dark, curly hair. It was easy for me to spot her at the film and screenwriting gatherings we both attended in Boulder, Colorado. All I had to do was find Waldo's hair, if you will. And I looked for her, mostly because, even from her vantage point beneath the sea of talking heads, she exuded sincerity, lack of pretense, and an eagerness that matched my own.

Prior to meeting each other, we had separately explored the Boulder screenwriting scene, which was slowly growing. Walk down your block today and you'll find someone who has a screenplay in mind, if not one completed and on its way to Hollywood (electronically, of course). But not back then. In fact, I'd had to find out how to write a screenplay by going to the library (*the library!*) and reading archaic material on the subject, giving rise to one of the most amateurish pieces of writing I ever put my name to. I even paid someone to create an illustration for the front cover, as if to advertise my lack of professionalism right from the get-go. Live and learn. (Which could have been an alternative title for this book.)

Still, I persisted, and managed to find an amazing mentor, a handsome, rugged, and talented old guy from another one of my screenwriting groups who was kind enough not to laugh at my work. Unlike the loudest critics in that particular screenwriting group, he could actually write, and one day, he greeted me with an understanding smile and a 30-page handwritten critique of that first screenplay. The kind that actually inspires you rather than making you want to flush your script down the toilet and plunge in after it.

The epiphany that screenwriting was an option, albeit a long shot as a career, hit me a couple of years prior to my meeting Kim. It's so hard for me to believe, looking back, that I hadn't a clue how movies got made, despite the fact that I loved them and that, sleet or snow, my husband and I went to the movies together every Friday night. Nor did I know that a movie blueprint was called a screenplay, and that some lucky bugger assumed the task of writing it. In my blissful ignorance, the film credits might as well have been written in Mandarin. Nor did I stay to watch them scroll by.

Then, one day, I was asked to write a video script for the computer software company (one of the first of its kind) I worked for in Chicago. *A script? Say what?* I did some research (minus the Internet, not yet available to the common woman), wrote the script, rented a camera of substantial proportions (I mean big), and shot the video. And suddenly, I realized in a mind-blowing flash (that belated epiphany) that someone had actually written the blueprint for *The Princess Bride, Zulu, The Great Dictator, When Harry Met Sally, Cinema Paradiso, Singin' in the Rain, Places in the Heart, North by Northwest, Out of Africa, The Man Who Would be King, It's a Wonderful Life, Witness, Moonstruck,* and a host of other favorites. Screen credits now jumped out at me as if the Rosetta Stone had suddenly morphed into English before my very eyes.

Ow!

Now that I knew that screenwriters (and myriad other filmmaking players as well) existed in the flesh and not just as hieroglyphics on the screen, an entire world had opened up to me. I wanted to know every inch of it, every nuance, and would gladly have paid to intern on a film set just to learn the ropes.

Given the scarcity of film activity in our area at the time, I concluded that if I wanted to learn everything there was to learn, I would have to find a way to do it myself. Anyway, even if we could have afforded it (we couldn't), school wasn't an option. If there were any viable film schools at the time, none of them was close to home. And, besides, I had four children who ranged in age from 8 to late teens, all of whom needed my presence and attention.

Moving to California, then (and to a lesser degree, still) the home of all things film, wasn't an option either – for a lot of reasons, not the least of which was because I didn't want to go. I love Colorado! Let me rephrase that. I love the mountains. I love the cloud formations. I love the feel of the air when the aspens start changing colors. If you tried to drag me away, my heels would dig into that dry, red soil and plant themselves there like two unmovable pine trees (although you might be able to lure me to the south of France for a get-away if you were willing to cover the air fare).

Kim (left), a third-generation Colorado native and Pam, a Colorado transplant with deep karmic roots - circa 1993

Kim, in the meantime, was working as a paralegal, writing screenplays of her own and doing stand-up comedy in her spare time. A little impatient with the groups we attended, which were fun and sometimes informative, but which didn't seem to be helping us further our goals, she too was ready for the leap of faith.

By this time, I had written a number of fairly viable screenplays, a few of which were more than writing exercises. In fact, one of them had landed me a Hollywood agent. Still pretty naïve about how things worked in the business (sometimes that's a good thing), I had, in my mind's eye, cast Richard Farnsworth as Orville, the protagonist of (the once-entitled) *Too Old to Tango*, at the time one of my more viable screenplays. I had seen Mr. Farnsworth in *The Grey Fox*, had found him very, what's the word? – foxy – and was totally under his spell. I managed to find out who his agent was and called her up, having absolutely no idea what I was going to say when, and if, she picked up the phone. Our conversation went something like this:

                    ME
Hi. Is this Diane?

                    DIANE
Yes, it is.

                    ME
Hi, Diane. My name is Pam Nelson, and I'm calling because I understand you represent the actor, Richard Farnsworth…?

                    DIANE
That's right.

                    ME
Well, I've written this script called "Too
Old to Tango." And… well, I really think
Mr. Farnsworth would be perfect in the
lead role. Actually, I wrote the script with
him in mind.

                    DIANE
Are you a producer?

                    ME
A producer? No! No. I'm not. I just think
he'd be perfect for the part. And I was
wondering if – well, I was wondering if
you'd be willing to get the script to him.
But, I mean, no. I'm not a producer.

                    DIANE
Well, I appreciate your thinking of
Richard. Unfortunately --

                    ME
But I mean, isn't there any way you could
get him to read the script? He'd be so
perfect.

I seemed to be stuck on the word "perfect".

                    DIANE
I'm sure he would.

Then the sigh that signaled concession, followed by the words I longed to hear.

> **DIANE**
> Go ahead and tell me a little about the story.

Amazingly, I'd actually prepared for this, and gave her the 25-words-or-less, which wasn't easy, given the fact that *Too Old to Tango* was what people in the industry like to call a *soft* story – that is to say, the antithesis of *high concept*[1].

A long pause.

> **DIANE**
> Tell you what. I'll fax you a release form. Just sign it and send it back with the script. I'll give it a read.

It was apparently my lucky day. Diane was what was called a packaging agent. If she found a script she really liked, she worked on putting the elements together, i.e., by attaching a producer, a director, or maybe an actor or two.

I sent her the script and soon thereafter got a call from her, expressing her enthusiasm for the material and saying that she wanted to represent me. My contract followed quickly by Fed-Ex.

By the time Kim and I threw our hats into the ring, I had reasons to be optimistic about the possibilities of my new avocation/career. Here's why:

- Screenplay story ideas[2] flowed, nay gushed, from... well, from wherever they come, and I had by then, written at least a dozen scripts, among them, *A Bucket of Paint* – specifically written as a low-budget film. I was getting better at my craft.

- My agent had tentatively lined up a Canadian (as I remember) producer for *Too Old to Tango* and was also pitching a couple of my other scripts.

- Someone from Sundance had called to let me know I was a contender for their screenwriting lab (I didn't make the final cut). I was also doing well in other screenwriting contests.

- Sidney Poitier's production company said they would add me to their "writer's list", based on another screenplay. (Nothing ever came of that, but the positive feedback was appreciated, and my one remaining screenwriting group was duly impressed.)

- More than one well-known producer had expressed an interest in another of my favorite (animation and live action feature) screenplays.

There would be many other such expressions of interest in my work, though nothing substantial ultimately came of any of them. Sometimes you just have to say, *C'est la vie*. And then you have to pick up the pace.

———

Kim sat in front of me at the Women in Film-Denver's[3] meeting that day, and I waited impatiently for the meeting to end before tapping her on the shoulder and asking if we could talk. It quickly became clear that we were of the same mind and that making a movie was definitely at the top of her to-do list. I suggested *A Bucket of Paint* and she took the script home to read it.

There we stood, at the intersection of brave and foolhardy, chomping at the bit to take the leap into the unknowable void. Had we been able to foresee the future, would we have done anything differently? Of course, we would have! But for now, blind to what was to come, we thought only of forging ahead. Fueled by the joy of immersing ourselves in what we loved most, we knew only that we had the will, the faith, and the eagerness to turn our dreams into something magical. Did we know we were taking chances? Yes. And no. In theory, we knew things could go wrong. In actuality, we'd never been to that part of town and couldn't imagine the terrain. Simply put, failure was not only not an option – it wasn't even a glimmer on the horizon of our imaginations.

From Kim:

Many years ago, in my college communications course, we were asked to write down what we wanted to do in the future. Though I was a vocational education major at the time, I wrote down that I wanted to have my own film production company. Well, instead, I became a paralegal – a paralegal whose spare time was spent acting, doing voice work, stand-up comedy, improv and screenwriting. I was also a volunteer camera operator on local cable shows and eventually produced, directed and wrote some comedy bits and legal videos.

Years later, at a Women in Film meeting, we were asked to state our goals in film. Both Pam and I expressed our desire to make a feature film. We had always gravitated toward each other at these functions, as we shared similar thoughts and philosophies. Having met my share of people who were full of themselves, I found Pam to be refreshing and a delight to talk to about film and other matters.

Immediately following the meeting, we exchanged ideas and decided we should make a film together! I was elated… first, because the opportunity of making a film had finally presented itself, and second… I was going to be working with Pam!

Both Pam and I had business backgrounds, as well as an irrepressible creative side. Granted, neither one of us had any experience putting together a feature film, but our business experience, combined with Pam's wonderful script, made for exciting possibilities.

To our delight, we discovered that people were drawn to our project, and the dream, as it were, quickly began moving toward reality. We were going to make a feature film! Could there be anything more exciting?

1 – There is no one definition of a "high concept" script. Some say it's any story that can be pitched in a single sentence, but this isn't entirely accurate, as sometimes a "softer" idea can also be pitched in one sentence (it probably won't, however, sound terribly exciting). It might then be more accurate to say that in the case of a "high concept" script, the premise of the film *and* its marketing potential can be conveyed in a sentence or two. A "soft" script, on the other hand, depends more heavily on character, dialogue, and other, less marketable factors, the full potential of which can't easily be conveyed in a short pitch.

2 – Though my DNA must point to a strong affinity for writing, I was also cursed at birth with two writing impediments. The first was a virtual absence of story ideas, and the second was the inability to finish anything I started. One day, in my twenties, I decided to challenge my two-pronged karma by writing a novel from some meagre, un-novel-worthy idea, and then finishing the story no matter how deeply my heart and my fingers resisted. I hated that story all the way to its bitter and merciful end, somewhere around 300 pages – at which point, victoriously but unceremoniously, I threw the whole shebang into the trash. From that moment on, I was never short of ideas. And I learned to cherish each one that came my way as if it were manna from the heavens. Never again did I have a problem finishing anything I started.

3 – Kim and I were founding members of the Denver Chapter. I was later a Vice President (of the Denver Chapter) for one term. The chapter later dissolved – there may not have been enough interest – only to return with gusto in 2016, no thanks to us, but much to our delight.

LAUNDRY ROOM OPERATIONS
Is that my Uncle Flying Past the Window?

June 1993 *—As much as we'd love to move into a real office, it's not something we can afford right now, much the less justify. Sometimes you just have to make do with what you've got. And what we've got is an undersized laundry room.*

I was still working for that start-up computer software company in the Chicago area when Lauren (my husband), and I decided to make the move to Colorado. Knowing how much we loved Colorado[1], Lauren's ex-boss, who had already moved this way, offered him a job in Denver. Now, if we could only figure out what to do about *my* income, there was a real possibility we could make the move.

My then-boss and owner of the company made it easy for me when he offered to set me up working out of my home once we moved. I could no longer act as the training director, but I could still oversee documentation, which was good enough for me. A hookup by modem to Chicago's mainframe computer and an occasional trip to Chicago were all that would be required. I was beyond grateful for his willingness to accommodate me.

We packed up and made the move, finding it tough to leave our friends behind but, otherwise, pretty excited to start this new chapter of our lives.

All went well, though it was hard to find a workable place to set up that home office in our new house. It had to be in close proximity of the kids, but also afford me the privacy and seclusion needed to actually be able to concentrate. My father quickly got on it, converting what had been the main floor laundry room into a usable office space – usable, but barely able to accommodate one person – let alone a computer, phone and fax machine. The room was, in fact, about the size of a very small walk-in closet, so small, in fact, that I found myself having to open the door to ventilate the room every seven minutes to keep from passing out. There was a small window in the office, but oddly enough, even wide open, it neither let in the good air, nor let out the bad.

When the kids were at school, I kept things more breathable by leaving the door open, which turned out to be an actual life-saver when I left oil heating up on the burner and our smoke alarm battery was dead. FYI, reading fire extinguisher instructions well before the critical moment is highly recommended.

The Chicago-Colorado telecommuting job didn't last all that long, but my converted laundry room office remained, and it would go on to serve as the production office for *A Bucket of Paint* for longer than either Kim, or I, might have wanted.

Aside from breathability, there were other issues with that office. While Kim and I never made any attempts to present ourselves as anything or anyone other than who we were – that is to say, two women, managing to get by, who wanted badly to make a feature film and were working hard to make it happen -- we did try to act with as much professionalism as possible. In other words, being real was one thing; painting an especially vivid picture of reality was another – that vivid reality being me calling from a 4' x 3' laundry room, kids bouncing off the walls in the adjacent room, dogs barking madly at anything that threatened to move across the front lawn. Not exactly the picture of your Hollywood mover and shaker.

In anticipation of particularly important phone calls, I would pre-emptively ask children and animals to hold it down, but would also follow that up with stuffing an assortment of towels at the bottom of the office door in an effort to muffle any especially high-decibel sounds – then pray no one came along to ring the doorbell. I really hated making those phone calls, but there was no way around it. I had no cell phone (did anyone?). The landline was in my office, and I had to make the best of it.

This little corner of suffocating space was, alternately, a production office and a writing room, as well as a refuge in the way that sticking your head under a pile of covers is a refuge – and just about as oxygen-depriving.

One day, as I sat at my computer, typing away, I thought I saw something flash by that useless window. My father and uncle, both in their eighties at the time, were in the process of installing a whole-house swamp cooler for us, and I figured one of them must have dropped (or thrown) a tool down from the roof. Satisfied with this explanation, I continued typing. Ten minutes later, my uncle stoically labored in from the back yard, stopped by my office door long enough for me to take in the gray-green hue of his skin, and asked:

"Where's Kenny?"

"Well," said I with a measure of uncertainty, "he's up on the roof with... you?"

Is it a bird? Is it a screwdriver?
No, it's my uncle!

Which was when my uncle announced with ill-placed panache that he'd fallen off the roof (a good fifteen foot fall onto a bed of rocks). Being the resilient, intrepid men they both were – oh, those fearless men of yore! – my uncle and father insisted that marinating my uncle in a bath of cold water, rather than taking him to the emergency room, was the thing to do. A long, cold soak and they were back on the roof, tying themselves to the nearly-installed swamp cooler for safekeeping. If you can call it that.

How I could have mistaken my uncle flying past my window for a screwdriver, I'll never know. Now, when I conjure up the memory, it's him I see, not the screwdriver. I see myself up on that roof too, Kim at my side, tied to that swamp cooler for dear life. There's a parallel there, and I'm not blind to it.

1 – I went to school in Colorado, my parents retired here, and the annual family reunion was spent skiing and playing tennis. In Colorado, you could do both on the same day.

VELVET

Driving Through Roswell, New Mexico with an Alien in the Passenger Seat

January 1994 *– I'm not sure film festivals are really the best place to drum up financial support for a project still in development, but here we are at Sundance, trying to drum up support for a project still in development. Suffice it to say that we haven't gotten anywhere, but on the way to nowhere, we've met a lot of interesting people.*

One of the more interesting people we met at Sundance that year was Velvet. At the time, we were considering Howard Keel for a key role, as music was, and would remain, a big component of the film. We attended a panel of some sort – can't remember exactly what it was, except that it had something to do with music – film scoring, maybe? Anyway, we milled around afterward, talking with this person and that person, when a young woman, having overheard the gist of one of our casual conversations, broke in to introduce herself.

"Hi. I'm Velvet."

More ominous words were never spoken. (Except maybe, "Hi, I'm Candi." But more on that later.)

Velvet was gorgeous. Great skin. Thick, black hair. A resplendent, ear-to-ear smile. Perfect teeth. All in all, she smacked of healthy genes. And, after nudging more details out of us (an easy task), she seemed sincerely interested in our film, which, in our minds, was further testament to the superiority of her genes.

I jest. But not about her interest in our film. She wanted to be part of it. Somehow. Some way. Perhaps she could find us an investor. She had lots and lots of contacts.

"Here's my card. Call me. I know people. We'll talk soon. After the festival. I'll be back in Texas. Call me at home."

Maybe it wasn't quite that staccato, but the message was clear. *I can help.*

"Great!" An interested party – with connections. Lots and lots of them. Hey – maybe an up-close look at Hugh Grant wasn't all we were going to get out of this festival!

(Actually, now that I think of it, Hugh Grant was the year before. That year, the Grand Jury Award went to Edward Burns for *The Brothers McMullen*, a film with an Irish bent, as was ours. As we stood in line to get into the Awards Ceremony, we chatted with Mr. Burns, comparing notes, and applauding him on his film, which we had made a point of seeing, staying for the Q&A that followed, and falling quite enamored with the charming young filmmaker from New York.)

Kim and I left the film festival in good spirits, and returned to Denver and reality to continue peddling our wares. After what seemed like a reasonable interval, I picked up the phone and called Velvet. She answered right away and, like a skilled doctor who knows just how to cure what ails you, dutifully gave us the needed infusion of hope that money was waiting around the corner. We were already beyond the sitting around waiting for anyone stage, or the holding your breath stage – so after I hung up, we went ahead with our work, putting Velvet's enthusiastic assurances on the back burner, if not the back porch.

Don't count on anyone. Just keep working at it. We'll believe it when we see it. That was pretty much our mantra. Let it be noted for posterity that these are healthy words to live by.

Then, one day, many months later, our new Co-Producer, Gloria, whom we had met through Women in Film, mentioned that she happened to be on her way to Austin (or some such city in Texas) for reasons that had little or nothing to do with the film. Remembering that Velvet lived in the neighborhood, I suggested Gloria give her a call. No harm in following up, but again, we weren't holding our breath.

So Gloria went to Texas.

And Gloria came back from Texas.

In a stolen moment, she called us to report on her trip, the essence of which (to the best of our recollection) follows:

Not long after arriving in Austin, Gloria gave Velvet a call and explained who she was with relationship to the film. Velvet seemed happy to hear from her. We assume, but don't remember now, that they then met in person. At any rate, when Gloria was ready to return to Denver, Velvet asked if she could catch a ride with her. This seemed a little presumptuous to Gloria and was a little unsettling as well, given that she really didn't know this individual, nor did she quite comprehend why she wanted to hitch a ride to Denver, though it seemed to have something to do with our film. Nevertheless, in the interest of supporting the film, Gloria agreed to give her a lift.

It wasn't until night fell and they were traveling through (or in close proximity to) Roswell, New Mexico, that Velvet decided the moment was right to inform her that she (Velvet) was in fact a *walk-in*. This begged an explanation, which Velvet provided, explaining that *walk-ins* are spirits that take over and inhabit the bodies of deeply compromised individuals (which was apparently the case with the original Velvet).

Now, you have to hand it to Gloria for remaining calm in a squeamish situation, i.e., driving through Roswell, New Mexico with an alien in the passenger seat (with a long way to go to daylight and Denver). But Gloria somehow managed, and the two made it safely to Gloria's front door – because, by then, Velvet (despite her walk-in status, we'll still call her Velvet) had inveigled her way into staying at Gloria's for an extended sleep-over. What are you going to say when an alien invites herself for a sleep-over – *no*?

Not only did Velvet want to spend a couple of nights, she seemed to have no intention of leaving – or, at least, Gloria couldn't find an easy way to get rid of her. At odd hours of the night, Gloria would hear Velvet on the phone, urgently whispering away, as if plotting the takeover of Planet Earth. Understandably, Gloria wasn't happy with the situation, and she asked if we could meet with Velvet to let her know her film-related services (whatever Velvet thought they were) would not be required.

We planned a luncheon date for the four of us at a nice restaurant where forks and knives would be readily available.

Kim and I had no idea what to expect. Had Gloria inadvertently hooked up with the wrong person – Velvet's wacky roommate, maybe? But one look at Velvet seated at the table told us this was the same person we had met at Sundance. Well, at least the shell was the same. Same hair, same teeth, same body. And yet, as we quickly discovered, her personality was completely different. Where the original Velvet had been charming, warm and intelligent, this edition of Velvet was dark and intimidating, and utterly lacking in the charm and intellect of the original. It was freaky, to say the least.

I was charged with telling her we wouldn't be needing her for the film in any way whatsoever, funding included. An extra-terrestrial investor was really out of the question. So, please – order what you will from the menu, but this is pretty much the part where you go back to where you came from.

Suffice it to say, this didn't sit well with Velvet, who fought us with angry eyes and cutting words (but not forks and knives), forcing us to take a very hardline position:

"Check, please!"

I have to admit that Kim and I were a little uneasy after that. In time, however, Velvet faded from the recesses of our minds, and not long after that luncheon, she packed up and left Gloria's house, which was undoubtedly a great relief for Gloria.

Only years later would Velvet resurface in our lives – not as a human, or as an alien, but as the general concept for a campy, sci-fi romantic comedy called, *Walk-ins Welcome*.

SHOE IN THE ROAD
The Office on Squirrel Street

January 1994 *– We've applied with the Secretary of State for corporate status under the name, Shoe in the Road Productions Inc. We're now an official corporation! Here's what our logo/letterhead looks like:*

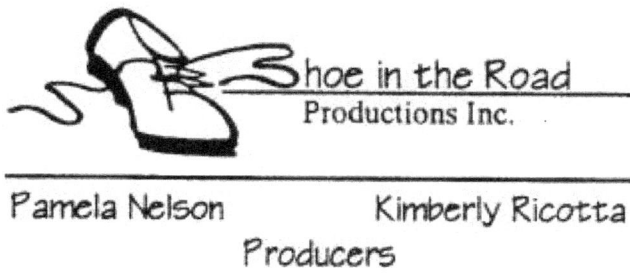

It's hard to exaggerate the sense of elation Kim and I were feeling as we made our way forward in the direction of our mutual dream. In fact, elation seemed to grease the way for us, to make the task seem virtually effortless – though, looking back, it certainly wasn't. But it was a joyous process – and joy, in and of itself, can make the going seem easy.

The time had now come to cement our partnership and our existence as a production entity. To concretize the ephemeral and make reality of the fantasy. To declare without equivocation that *A Bucket of Paint* was going to *be*.

But what would we call this new entity that would propel our film into existence?

We went through the dictionary, threw words at each other over the kitchen table, spent hours in futile-but-fun, chocolate-munching brainstorming. Nothing. And then, we drove down the street, passed a shoe in the road, and that was it.

Shoe in the Road became our corporate umbrella, under which we hoped to develop many projects to come, beginning, of course, with our first feature film, *A Bucket of Paint*.

First order of business: finding ourselves a good entertainment attorney. Not easy to do in Denver at that time. They just weren't around. We did locate a really nice lawyer who was loosely affiliated with film, but only beginning to dip his toes into the water. Given the shortage of Denver entertainment attorneys, a toe-dipper would probably have been okay with us – but this one didn't feel ready to take us on and respectfully declined.

A short time later, an industry acquaintance recommended an entertainment attorney licensed in New York, where so much of the *A Bucket of Paint* project would naturally gravitate. This attorney really seemed to know his business (which happened to be show business), and had a relaxed, fun-loving streak that appealed to us. *Chill* could have been his middle name, and since all he could do for us until further notice was chill, we figured it was a good fit.

Marty was jovial, smart, and good at what he did. Eventually, we sealed the deal.

And thus it was that *Shoe in the Road* was born, and Marty hired to protect its interests.

Not long after this, we started looking in earnest for a real production office. Eventually, we would find one – or, I should say, Lauren (my husband) would find one, through a painting contact of his. We loved the building, which was sweet and unimposing and surrounded by an abundance of mature trees that served to keep the heat down inside. Squirrels were so prevalent in the trees outside the windows that it was downright distracting. You couldn't help looking out your window, wondering, *What are they up to now?* It was easy to put all ambitions aside, at least momentarily, in favor of watching their crazy antics. Ergo, we fondly remember the place as the *Office on Squirrel Street*.

Best of all, it was the perfect size – just enough room for two desks, two phones, some filing cabinets, a fax machine, and some books, with room to get up and stretch. There was a lobby too, which served another adjacent office as well as our own. Best of all, there was a deli across the street. And it was cheap – the office, that is. The deli too, for that matter. And you could rent the office by the month if you needed to. About the only issue we ever encountered there was that someone on the premises smoked, and sometimes the second-hand smoke would seep its way into our office – or, at least, the smell of it would. It was the only disadvantage to an otherwise perfect place.

I think it's safe to say that at this point Kim and I were feeling pretty positive about things. Not to mention well-fed. Sometimes we'd just sit at our desks, relishing some deli concoction or other, and stare at each other knowingly from across the room. Even in the silence, the exhilaration was palpable. We were going somewhere. Somewhere exciting. Somewhere fun. Somewhere new and unexplored. And all without a compass or a road map to guide us.

THE FACE OF A BRIEFCASE
What More Could Two Girls Ask For?

January 1994 *– The more we know, the more we know we don't know, as the saying goes. It's obvious we're going to need to put together a workable budget. Eventually, we'll need help with various aspects of pre-production. Whomever we bring on board should also function as the key manager during production of the film, reporting to us at the end of the day. But that's down the road. Right now, what we need is a viable budget. Putting one together is the next big step and we'll need some help with that from someone who's been there before.*

Going down the list of candidates (a fairly short one), we made calls, asked what we thought were pertinent questions, and narrowed the search to a couple of potential line producers capable of putting together a film budget.

Our notes at the time regarding our phone conversation with Ronald DeLong, who would become our chosen Line Producer, indicated that he had once held the position of Interim Film Commissioner and that, parenthetically, he had a nice voice. You can sometimes tell a lot from the quality and texture of someone's voice over the phone. At other times, it doesn't mean a thing. We made an appointment to interview him at a local coffee shop.

Kim and I sat across from each other in a booth, waiting for Ron to arrive, which he did in a timely fashion. My first reaction to him wasn't to *him*, but to the briefcase he carried and placed beside him on the seat as if it were joining us for coffee. The briefcase was old and worn – the yellowish-brown of a faded leather – not faux though. Just falling apart.

My brain went three directions with this. First, shock and awe: *Wow! That briefcase has seen it all!* followed by a warm feeling of kinship, *This guy can't let his briefcase go – I can totally relate to that!* and finally, downright pity, *Well, if things go really well, maybe Ron can finally afford a new briefcase, and wouldn't that be nice?"*

Whatever the case, Ron's briefcase seemed to speak louder than Ron, although I wasn't sure what it was actually saying. I still liked Ron's voice, though, and he had a nice enough presence. I forced myself to focus on Ron's face, which I saw as both convivial and unremarkable, and not on the face of his briefcase.

In a calm, almost plodding manner and backed by a plethora of stories illustrating his skill and experience as both a Producer and Line Producer, Ron inspired us to a certain level of confidence. Doing due diligence wasn't as quick and easy a process as it might be today – but if he'd once been hired as an Interim Film Commissioner, wasn't that already a meaningful vote of confidence?

We seemed to hit it off well enough, Kim and Ron and I. Coffee was good, conversation pleasant. Ron's briefcase faded into insignificance as Ron asserted his own significance into our quest. And so, with just a little more due diligence and only a little apprehension, we welcomed our new Line Producer on board.

Actually, to say we welcomed him on board might be a stretch, as we had no money at that point to pay him, though we would quickly put together enough money to have him flesh out the first draft of a working budget. At this point, he was simply "attached", becoming part of the package we were assembling to try to raise production money. While Kim and I ran around town, attended festivals, and made calls in an effort to secure "the money", Ron put some efforts of his own into the same quest – a welcome gesture which might have, in the end, served us all (but didn't).

One contact Ron made was with a guy named Jake. Jake was something of a money finder, a go-between, if you will. He liked the script and wanted to send it to a production entity that he thought might well be interested in our project. The script was duly sent out and, not long after, Jake came back to Ron, telling him that his "people" wanted to know if we had other scripts. If so, they'd like to see them. But this time, they wanted top sheets attached. A top sheet is the cover page (or pages) for the budget, giving the breakdown and a grand total at the bottom. Budget details are covered in the actual budget, but in this case, just the top sheet for each script would do.

Kim and I decided to give him / them three other scripts – one a live action and animation romantic comedy; one a high concept action drama; and one a dramedy. Ron offered to put together the requested top sheets, which we were glad to let him do, given the fact that we'd never done one before. There were no detailed budgets to summarize, so the top sheet numbers would have to be educated estimates. Ron felt he could put together something viable.

In short order, the scripts and top sheets went out and we waited to hear back. In the meantime, the quest for money to produce *A Bucket of Paint* continued.

———

The budget, according to Ron's feedback, wasn't going to be all that small. That is, not if we wanted to do it right. Not if we wanted actors we could bank on. Not if we wanted wider distribution and a successful film. All of which sounded good to us.

While it was great to have a line producer attached to our project, especially one who seemed almost as eager as us to get that money rolling in, Kim and I now felt the need to enlist the services of a business consultant. Although the two of us felt pretty comfortable in the business world, the ins and outs of a potentially million-dollar-or-more project were, at this point in our experience, a little out of our league. A good friend pointed us in the direction of Bob, a successful businessman himself, and a man who now made a business out of proffering hard-earned advice.

We met Bob at a sweet little café in the suburbs, where, as it turned out, we would meet with him time and time again, through thick and thin, joy and sorrow. Bob was solid, tall, handsome, affable. A golfer and a guy's guy. His hair was a shade of gray that complemented his frequent tan and reinforced his overtly masculine and take-charge persona. Bob was sharp too. Nothing seemed to get by him. He dispensed advice both deliberately and sparingly. While he made an art of listening to you, he also made sure you listened to him when it came his turn to speak. He weighed his every word and, whether you made sense of it or not, whether you agreed with it or not, you knew it behooved you to put down your coffee and listen up. We liked him right away. We think he liked us.

So now we had a business consultant, someone who loomed almost larger-than-life and exuded savvy and stature and self-assurance.

Ron, Marty and Bob. What more could two girls ask for?

NO TIME FOR THE GIGGLES
A Gallic Dinner with our Director

April 1994 – *One of my dear friends, Sue, has stepped up to the plate to become one of our first development investors, enabling us to fly our almost-chosen Director to Denver for an informal dinner meeting. Needless to say, we can't wait to meet him.*

Kim and I sat at our table in a pleasant and aromatic French restaurant, eagerly awaiting Ron's and Nigel's arrival. When I say *eagerly*, I mean that Nigel's imminent arrival had taken precedence in my mind over the panoply of Gallic menu offerings in front of my face, and I could barely think to order a glass of cabernet. On second thought, better to wait on that glass of wine, lest I kill the brain cells responsible for my best vocabulary, or find myself collapsing into a fit of ill-placed giggles.[1]

By the time our lives intersected with Nigel's that night, I had pretty well mastered the art of stifling the giggles, but it's a proven fact that wine can unleash the monster, so… no wine for me. At least not until all the parties were present and others were, in their own unique ways, equally affected.

My first impression upon seeing Nigel walk in was that he had a certain *presence*, an easy-going self-confidence that matched his casual, but purposeful, stride. He walked and talked, secure in who he was and where he was going. Which, in this case, was straight over to our table to amicably shakes our hands and bestow his warmest smile upon us before sitting down next to me and ordering that ice-breaking glass of wine in a velvety voice deeply infused with British accent.

Nigel was an acquaintance of Ron's. Based on work they had done together in the past (or so we understood), Ron felt that Nigel would be a good fit for our project. Kim and I studied our potential director now and, with every sip of wine, every bite of warm French bread smothered with pâté, we mutually reached the conclusion that we would be lucky to have him. Not because his English was lovely to listen to, nor because he was inescapably charming, but because he really seemed to know his stuff. More importantly, he seemed to possess the humor and sensitivity required to direct this film. And it didn't hurt, of course, that he had already won an Academy Award, a couple of Emmys, and other significant awards and accolades. (The Oscar was for a beautiful documentary that he had directed just a few years back.) By the end of the evening, Kim and I were elated. Nigel loved the project. We loved Nigel.

We had ourselves a Director!

Come what may (and many things did come), we never lost our faith in Nigel's ability to do justice to our film. Nor did he ever prove himself to be anything short of a fine human being and capable Director. In so many ways, *A Bucket of Paint* and Nigel held the promise of a match made in film heaven.

1 - Giggles have been a recurring curse in my life, always seeming to overtake me at the least propitious moments and for the most ridiculous of reasons. My brother Johnny was equally afflicted. Once, in grade school, we were sent to the principal's office for inciting the school bus to raucous behavior. Sheepishly, we looked up at the principal as she scolded us. Her eyelashes spiraled at the ends like hairy helixes, and scold us as she might — and did — her words were obscured by the whooshing of those never-ending lashes. We stole a glance at each other and were instantly lost, bursting into laughter that had no end, which is what happens, of course, when you get a bona fide case of the giggles. The angrier our poor principal got, the weaker with laughter we became. In the end, there was simply no threat of punishment to rival our misplaced merriment.

FINDING THE FINDER
How a Painter's Eavesdropping Paid Off

November 1994 *– We can't make a movie without money and we don't have any big money connections to speak of – most of the people we know are either broke, just making do, or doing just fine but not in a position to finance what, according to Ron's budget calculations, is now turning out to be a multi-million-dollar production. It's been months, and our noses for money are taking us nowhere. We need to find a finder.*

Lauren (my husband) used to paint houses as a second job. It seemed to take three jobs for us to support ourselves and our four children – my steady job of the moment, his job as a route salesman, and then his second job as a part-time painter. Occasionally, I would help him out on a job, to save a little money, but mostly just so we could be together, together-time being a precious commodity.

One time, on an interior job, after I had just gotten an über-short haircut, donned a painter's cap, a man's white collared shirt, white painting pants, and dipped my paint brush into the paint pan, I noticed some guy staring at me through the sliding patio door. I was finally compelled to open it (he seemed innocent enough). He studied me a little more closely, his eyes landing and lingering on my chest, and then asked, "Are you a boy or a girl?" As we later discovered, he was mentally and emotionally challenged, which may have accounted for his courage and honesty in asking. Good question, I ruminated. What *was* I doing in a man's painting outfit? And how the hell did we really expect to raise money – big money – for this film, given our own financial situation? Now, maybe our own financial circumstances didn't really matter. After all, we weren't investing our own money.

But on certain days, at certain moments (i.e., with someone questioning my very essence through a patio door), our lack of financial stability felt deeply, darkly relevant.

By this time, I had left behind my steady job, though still picking up a few bucks here and there writing resumes and doing other odd writing jobs. I had also taken on a part-time job typesetting checks for a check printing company. I was both fast and dyslexic, though not fatally so. With regard to our film, I chose to be totally forthright with my employers during my interview, telling them that, as soon as we had found our financing, I would be leaving them for more verdant pastures. They were remarkably fine with this, maybe because they figured it would be a cold day in hell (and not terribly verdant) before we got the money. Or maybe they figured that my typesetting skills were pretty replaceable. On the other hand, they were so kind and supportive, I think they actually believed we would succeed – maybe even sincerely hoped we would.

Meantime, Kim and I were trying to drum up interest in our film. We talked to a lot of people – mostly people who liked to talk, but also people who wanted to meet us out of sheer curiosity ("Wow! You guys are really going to make a movie?"). Or people who didn't have anything to contribute but thought you might be able to help *them* in some way ("I have a great idea for a movie – do you want to hear it?") Finally, there were those who showed up for the free Red Robin dinner, wiped their chins, and wished us good luck. And those who didn't show up at all.

We even found *finders* who, we hoped, would lead us to the millions we needed. We have nothing negative to say about any finder we happened to meet in the course of our quest. Finding film money was just not their forte and, apart from liking to talk, wanting to satisfy a certain curiosity, wondering if you'd like to hear their idea for a movie, and having a keen appreciation for Red Robin burgers, they really didn't have much to contribute. But, really, thank you anyway.

During my official ten-minute break from non-stop typing, I would check in with Kim. *Anything new?* Then I'd check in with my husband. *I thought I'd make some kind of casserole with that leftover chicken. Sound okay?* Unable to check in with the kids (who were all in school), I would check in with myself on their behalf. *Am I a good Mom? Will my children forgive me for not being around as much as I should – as much as I'd like to be?*

I told myself that if we were successful with this project, everyone in our family would benefit, including some good friends and maybe even some distant relatives, and we'd go for that long dreamed-of extended family vacation (minus some of the friends and distant relatives). And Lauren, our beloved mainstay, would get to quit painting once and for all. I pictured myself retiring his painting jersey by having that stiff, Pollock-like, paint-spattered shirt of his professionally framed and, with much pomp and ceremony, hanging it over the couch just so.

On the other hand, if we failed…

But, really, we couldn't think about that. How could we? In the case of something so daunting – the impossible dream, if you will – you can't move forward on the wings of imagined failure. Better just to take flight and believe. Better to just keep flapping those wings and not look down.

―――

Before launching into the project in earnest, Lauren and I talked about the risks involved. The problem is, you can talk about the risks all you want to – the fact is, you have no idea what the risks are until the ship's gone down. Then you're left in a leaky lifeboat with very few rations, surrounded by sharks, holding a water-logged compass, shouting obscenities at the sunset and the vagaries of existence. That's if you have a lifeboat, rations, and a compass and your throat's not too dry to shout. Sharks, you can count on. Not to mention thousands of miles of ocean and the vagaries of existence. (But more shipwreck analogies later...)

Still, we did our best to imagine a future in which, despite our best efforts, we didn't manage to reach our goal. How bad could it be? As I said before, it wasn't as if we were investing our own money. Lucky us – we had no money. Well, except for the money we might have been able to put in the bank had we opted for a more conventional future. That was certainly at risk. Beyond that, humiliation and disappointment seemed to loom as the most grievous possible outcomes, which we decided we could handle as long as went into it together and promised to stick by each other come what may. Lauren had faith in me. I had faith in my talent and willingness to work very, very hard. That seemed to us to be enough.

We held hands and took the family plunge. (Kim's official plunge would come a little later when she would lose her job at what happened to be the most fortuitous time for our project.)

Lauren became our avid supporter and self-appointed spokesperson for the film. He's a very likable guy, and while not exactly a social butterfly, he speaks from the heart and did so now to anyone who would lend a friendly ear.

Interestingly, however, when Lauren finally found our *finder* for us (say that ten times), it wasn't the result of a talking spree, but of an orgy of listening. And not so much a matter of listening as of eavesdropping. Like all good housepainters, he was a fly on the wall, painting the wall. And one day, his surreptitious listening skills paid off in a big way.

Kelly was a soft-spoken, unpretentious and sincere young man, maybe in his early thirties at the time, who worked from home. Lauren was painting one of the rooms in his house, just finishing the trim, when he overheard Kelly on the phone with a client. It didn't take long for Lauren to figure out that this guy was a finder – or, at least, was acting as such with his current client. Now, maybe film wasn't his forte. But it was worth a shot.

Kelly got off the phone and the fly on the wall buzzed in closer.

```
Pam's husband, Lauren,
    the painter
and fly on the wall.
```

```
             In those days,
his nickname was "Peach Boy".
```

The next thing we knew we had a face-to-face meeting with Kelly, a lover of film and believer in our project, who would become one of the most important and most genuine people we would come to meet in the course of putting the film together.

The fly had found the finder.

And the finder would find us the funds. (And thus ends my annoying run of alliteration – at least for the moment.)

———

Words can't possibly describe how excited Kim and I were to have found a qualified investor (we'll call her Joan) to fund our film. The truth is, when we set out to make a film, we had absolutely no idea how we were going to find the production money. Our attitude at the time was that we couldn't let that sticky wicket get in the way – otherwise, we would be thwarted at the onset. Instead, we figured that if we embarked on the journey, eyes fixed forward, never veering from the path, our will alone (the Japanese call it *ichinen*) would create opportunities for us. Things would somehow fall into place. And, somehow, with a lot of work, they did.

From the outset, Kim and I had begun putting together our "package", which was always in a state of evolution, but which at this point included ourselves, Ron, Nigel, Marty, along with various letters of support and recommendation, a synopsis of the script, as well as information about the project and how we intended to structure the investment deal. Though actors didn't factor in much at this point, our investor was less interested in actors than in the script itself and in the budget. She undoubtedly felt confident that, given the money, we could get the right actors.

Kelly (our finder) provided us with ample documentation and other substantiation regarding Joan's investment firm that unequivocally demonstrated her authenticity. She was a fan of the project partially because of its strong musical element and also because her interest in film was postured toward family entertainment. She had already funded several independent features. We soon got to know her polite, no-nonsense way of operating, and felt deeply grateful to have her in our court. We were especially excited that she had stipulated the right to first negotiations for our next two projects.

Joan didn't live in Colorado, but we spoke with her often on the phone, and eventually exchanged long faxes that detailed what the contractual agreement between us would be. As said, she loved the script and was good with the budget, which initially, stood somewhere around $2.7 million (and would eventually be driven higher, to around $3 million, and later, even more).

Coming to terms and working out contractual language would take time and a lot of back-and-forthing and we began working on it right away. While we couldn't move forward in any way that exceeded the money currently in our bank account, we could, nonetheless, start to breathe some life into the project. For example, we could legitimately scout for locations and seriously meet with potential actors and crew.

In flashes of sudden, soul-searing awareness, Kim and I realized we had accomplished the impossible. We had found the money (the millions!) to fund our film. Yes, Lauren had found the finder who found us the funds, but the script and the package had cemented the deal. On one hand, the whole thing didn't seem remotely real. More like something from which we would soon awaken, paint bucket and empty wallet still in hand. On the other hand, our good fortune seemed completely natural and totally as it should be. *A Bucket of Paint*'s cast of characters was all so real, so meant to be, that nothing short of movie magic could be its fate.

Or ours, for that matter.

GOING HOWARD-KEELING
Time-Traveling in a Gold-Plated Lexus

Taken from a card we received
from Howard Keel at Christmas.
What a face! What a guy!

April 1995 – *It's amazing how much legwork there is involved in getting a film off the ground. Time is flying by! We're seriously considering Howard Keel for the role of an old song and dance man with a permanent twinkle in his eye. In his heyday, Keel was said to be Clark Gable and Errol Flynn all rolled up into one yummy humanoid. Well, yeah, he was tall and handsome and fit and all that good stuff. But this guy could also sing!*

I don't remember the flight itself, but I do remember landing at the airport in L.A. and being met by Howard Keel's manager – let's call him Marv – a nice guy with a laid-back attitude and a shiny, smooth-riding, gold Lexus. I imagine we were supposed to be duly impressed with our mode of transport, and as a mother of four, I certainly was (but mostly because there didn't seem to be any French fries lingering between the seats).

There were three of us on this mission: Kim, Nigel (now part of our package) and I.[1]

Nigel sat in the front, Marv drove, and Kim and I sat in the back seat. The friendly chat centered on the reason for our visit – Howard Keel, the man himself. Marv, who had apparently known Howard for a good, long time, regaled us with stories of Kathryn Grayson, Frank Sinatra and a host of others who had played a meaningful part in Howard's personal and professional life. Our ears perked up, we listened and laughed. It was a good ride.

A good ride and a very long one.

Ever driven to Palm Springs? The sea of windmills is never-ending, dizzying and downright otherworldly. Tuning out Marv's story of the moment, I stared out the window, imagining us time-traveling through space in a winged Lexus on our way to the golden era of Hollywood musicals to meet the (now-aging) icon. This was going to be fun! That is, if the constant spinning of the windmills didn't have me throwing up where Marv's French fries might have been.

At the time, Howard was living at a golf resort, making it possible for him to frequently indulge in one of the great passions of his life – martinis. I mean, golf. He met us at the resort's restaurant and marched right past our eagerly-extended hands to reprimand Marv who was apparently behind schedule. I think Howard was getting hungry, though he'd taken care of the thirst factor with a few of those cherished libations. Marv now securely in his place (can't say that he seemed bothered by the rebuke), Howard turned to us, found our hands, and greeted us warmly. At 6' 4", he virtually towered over Kim, quickly swallowing up her hand in his. The smile, the sexy-even-at-his-age charm, the baritone voice, the twinkle in his eye. We were instantly hooked.

Well, I mean, Kim and I were.

In a strange turn of events, I – whose memory book is made up of a series of meals – cannot remember what I ate that day, though I imagine it was a salad of some sort. After all, I wasn't there for the food, was I? We talked – mostly Nigel and Howard – about Howard, about the part. I don't remember what Howard ate either, though I do remember the martinis that kept on a'comin' like an all-you-can-drink buffet. (Ask me the first thing that comes to my mind when you say "Howard Keel", and I'll say "olives". But then, his talent and the immensity of his persona quickly take a front row seat in my mind and the olives roll right off the plate.)

Howard had a great, hearty laugh, intimately tied to that robust voice of his. He laughed. We laughed, our laughter anemic by comparison to his – a couple of backup singers who could barely doo-wop. But we sure had fun that day at lunch with Mr. Showboat himself, just as I had imagined we would.

Well, at least Kim and I did.

Yet there was something a little strange about the overall atmosphere. The Oklahoma City bombing had just taken place the day before and, while the nation was reeling, we were, oddly enough, Howard Keel-ing. Yes, of course, life goes on. But Kim remembers excusing herself to go to the restroom at some point during the meal and being struck by the superficiality that seemed to dominate the restroom conversation. I mean, what can you expect in a restroom? Still, it seemed odd that no one appeared to know about, or care about, what was going on *out there*. At that exclusive resort restaurant, in Palm Springs, in the ladies' room, it was as if the Earth stood still.

At a moment of sudden quiet, Kim swears she heard someone whisper "Klaatu barada nikto"[1] from behind a stall door.

Not really. But if you're a sci-fi enthusiast, you'll get the point.

The meal ended. Howard reaffirmed his interest in the part. We shook hands again, took in Howard's smile for eternal safekeeping, and said our goodbyes.

Marv escorted us back to the car and drove us past the sea of windmills to the airport. This time I tried not to look outside.

The ride back was pretty much more of same, Marv regaling us with some great stories of an era gone by, Kim and I listening in from the back seat, and Nigel – what was Nigel doing, anyway? Seems he'd just borrowed Marv's cell phone (can't remember – had Nigel's battery died?) and was making a call, turning his head away from Marv as he awaited an answer from the other end, in an attempt to make things more private in a hopelessly public situation.

Despite Marv's delightful name-dropping narrative, Kim and I could pretty much hear what Nigel was saying. I guess he figured business was business (which Marv, if he was even tuned in, should appreciate), and that being the case, why waste time waiting for the perfect moment, especially when the perfect moment might be the present one? Whomever Nigel was calling (we assumed it was Charles Durning's agent) answered the phone.

As we would find out later, Charles Durning had read the script and was interested. And, in a nutshell, that's how the inimitable Howard Keel was replaced by the equally inimitable Charles Durning, while Kim and I sat in the back seat of a smooth-riding gold Lexus, watching the world spin by.

There is no denying that Charles Durning was absolutely, stunningly perfect for the part. Nigel must have known it and – perfect moment be damned – lost no time in calling the shot.

---

1 - If Ron was with us, we don't remember him. And, since decisions related to actors were not really his to make, we're going to conclude (right or wrong) that we can't remember him because he wasn't there. But then again…

CASTING & CRUMPETS
Does Life Get Any Sweeter Than This?

Oct. 6 1995 – *If you ask us, the most enjoyable part of putting a film together is casting, though not everyone will agree with us on this. As it turns out, some people actually dislike the process. But, come on, how fun is it to sit through an audition and watch a character come to life, sometimes in ways you never expected? Sitting there as unobtrusively as possible, nibbling on a scone, sipping on a cup of jasmine tea, listening, laughing, agonizing… does life get any sweeter than this? Only if you put honey in your tea!*

Things were moving along, the dream coming true before our eyes in ways we hadn't imagined, and suddenly a lot faster than we had anticipated. The search had begun for a Victorian house to use for filming exterior scenes. After eliminating a number of possibilities, Nigel decided on an enchanting Victorian, located on a quiet street in Boulder. Terms were worked out, and if all went right, we would be building a set to match that house, in which we would shoot the interior scenes, as well as some of the exterior scenes.

In the meantime, Nigel had been working on storyboarding.

Not really knowing how best to go about finding a Casting Director, Kim and I had (prior to finding our investor) decided to look for someone with an Irish-sounding name, for no better reason than that *A Bucket of Paint* leaned heavily toward the Irish. But before we could get Pat McCorkle on board, we had to pass the litmus test of a valued associate of hers, talent agent, Barry Douglas. As it turned out, he recommended the script to her, and that was how we were able to acquire a casting agent who turned out to not only have an Irish-sounding name, but a great reputation and a keen sense of casting.

Later, we met Barry in person in New York and loved him instantly. When he got word that we had found the money for the production of *A Bucket of Paint*, he sent us a beautiful bouquet of flowers. Barry passed away from AIDS some time later, but our memory of him is lasting. For Kim, whose own brother passed away from the same illness, Barry's passing was especially poignant.

Frances McDormand tentatively accepted a lead female role, but then pulled out for reasons having to do with personal commitments. Eventually, Mare Winningham, Julie Hagerty, Cyd Charisse, Jim True, Kevin O'Rourke, Charles Durning, Suzanne Bertish and the young, fresh-faced Drake Bell made up the ensemble cast.

Working in conjunction with a talented local Casting Director and our New York Casting Director, Nigel, Kim and I viewed live, as well as taped, auditions for roles not yet cast. Although we ultimately decided on Kevin O'Rourke for one of the remaining male leads, we all laughed heartily at John C. Reilly's taped audition, which Kim and I can still see in our mind's eye.

As the film's Director, Nigel had the final casting say. We had the utmost faith that Nigel's decisions would serve the film, so we were happy to give him veto power. His good instincts never let us down. He was innately an actor's director and very fond of his chosen actors. Suzanne Bertish and Mare Winningham were special choices for him, as was Julie Hagerty whom he called, after meeting with her for the role, a "great person – humane and delicate" – someone who connected "heart and soul" with the character.

The most difficulty we had was in casting Peter. Yes, it was an ensemble cast, but Peter was certainly, if not the protagonist, at least close to it. If his part wasn't as easy to cast as the other roles, it was mostly because, of all of *A Bucket of Paint's* characters, Peter was the least well-defined (as the writer, I was in touch with this fact). He was flawed, but then so were all the characters, so that really wasn't the issue. The issue was more that he was weak. But then he was supposed to be a little weak, at least at the onset. At any rate, if there was a flaw, it wasn't critical, and I figured this might have to be one of those cases of a gifted actor bringing dimension to a character who still needed a little fleshing out. (That being said, it's really the writer's job to flesh out the character to begin with.)

Before Pat McCorkle came on board, when Kim and I were putting out casting feelers, we had gotten in touch with Kevin Bacon, who turned down the part of Peter via a sweet, handwritten letter (now there's a classy guy) that was signed "your KB". "Your" was most probably supposed to be "yours" and, if we had gone to the pains of looking under a magnifying lens, we might have caught sight of a lingering "s" at the end of the word. But we had no intention of examining his writing under a magnifying lens; we just wanted to remember him as "our KB" which, with a smile, we still do.

At any rate, the part of Peter was turned down by a number of solid actors before Eric Stoltz tentatively accepted it after meeting with Nigel, only to turn it down when the projected shooting schedule proved to be too long. Ultimately, and to our delight, Jim True (now Jim True-Frost) accepted the part. In our minds (Kim's and mine and I venture to say, everyone else's), he was an ideal choice. He would inject both repressed Irishness and a comic twinkle that would be perfect for the part. Finally – we had our guy!

One day, early on, when Kim and I were returning calls from the office on Squirrel Street, I happened to speak with the agent of a well-known actor whom we were then considering for the part of Peter. The agent informed me that the actor wasn't available as he had just committed to a film, the title of which sounded strangely familiar to me. Hadn't I written just such a script – a script that had originally had that very title? Not only that, but wasn't the script in question one of the three that Ron had submitted some time ago to that unnamed production entity through the intermediary known as Jake? I was a little jarred at hearing this, but only briefly. In fact, I didn't have time to think about what similarities might exist between the scripts – this business is full of redundancy, right? – and I certainly didn't have the leisure to worry about it now. Instead, I squirmed briefly in my chair and moved on to the next phone call.

―――

Every actor attached to our project was, in our opinion, an absolutely perfect choice. Kim and I were especially excited at the prospect of working with Cyd Charisse. She was well into her seventies by now, but that was exactly what the part called for – an aging woman with sensational legs still raring to go underneath those crumpled panty hose.

Kim and I were (and still are) big fans of the old song and dance actors who were really the stars of our parents' generation. In my dreams, I work with them, I dance on stage with them, Gene Kelly holds me in his arms and sings to me. Who knows -- maybe the connection goes back to a past existence. If so, I was around for Vaudeville and for Chaplin too. Maybe I was an extra in his films or just hanging around the set, gawking and scrambling around, doing gofer work. The point is, both Kim and I feel a real attachment to those eras gone-by. And now, to be able to rub shoulders with a piece of the past in the form of the incomparable Cyd Charisse was something about which we were both very excited.

One day, on Squirrel Street, I spoke with Ms. Charisse on the phone. Although I don't remember the context of our conversation, I do remember the quality and inflection of her voice. "Oh, Pam…" she intoned, making three syllables, if not an entire melody, out of my name. In fact, she sounded a lot like my mother who in her later years used to leave phone messages for me that began much in the same way... "Oh, Paaaammmmm..."

Other exciting possibilities were brewing. At the Sundance Film Festival that year, Kim and I had seen *Out of Ireland*, a documentary featuring Mick Moloney, an Irish folklorist and musician. Impressed with Mr. Moloney's talents, we introduced ourselves to one of the film's Producers and later, *Shoe in the Road* would contact Mr. Moloney to talk to him about contributing his talents to our project.[1]

Lauren was excited about all of this too. For some reason, the Scandinavian in him is attracted to the Irish in others and, once introduced to the talents of Mick Moloney, he quickly decided he would one day join him on one of his personally guided, musically infused, tours of Ireland. (It's still on "my painter's" bucket list.)

Another musician about whose talents we were very excited was the American fiddler, Eileen Ivers. Nigel was especially eager to get her on board. Kim and I, Nigel, Ron and others had gone to see her perform one evening in Denver and were completely blown away.

We felt immensely privileged to think that she, Mick Moloney, and other gifted musicians, would lend their talents to our film. We'd also hooked up with an Irish dance school in Denver and made plans to use a few students to do an Irish stepdance in the film.

Add the talented Production Designer, Dan Leigh, and the wonderful Costume Designer, Susan Benson, to the mix, along with other crew who promised to be valuable assets to the film, and *A Bucket of Paint* was starting to come together in ways we couldn't have imagined a year or two ago. The tone, the feel, the texture of it was starting to crystalize into the promise of a very special film.

1 – In 1999, Mr. Moloney would go on to receive America's highest honor in the folk and traditional arts, the NEA National Heritage Fellowship.

SINGIN' IN THE RAIN WE'RE NOT
Air Cuts and the Fight Over Kim's Umbrella

June 1995 *– I've made a point of familiarizing myself with distribution deals, which are complicated, but strangely fascinating if you happen to like business jargon with a legal twist. Kim and I are in New York, on our way to FineLine Features to discuss potential distribution for* A Bucket of Paint. *It's a little early to be seeking a distribution deal – after all, we're still in the development stages – but, at the very least, we're intent on laying the foundation for the future. If the film turns out to be as good as we think it will be, we'll be able to come back to a receptive audience with a finished product that won't disappoint, and may be able to strike a good deal.*

FineLine isn't the only distribution company we're wooing. We're also in communication with October Films, Encore and Peacock, as well as exploring other possibilities.

New York, New York!
It's a wonderful town!
The Bronx is up and the Battery's down
The people ride in a hole in the ground…[1]

We wanted to look our best for our appointment with *FineLine Features* and decided to get haircuts at a salon conveniently attached to the large hotel in Times Square where we were staying. The salon was a little grander than what we were used to, and certainly a lot more expensive. To boot, clients and their stylists were on conspicuous display to pedestrians who walked by the windows in droves. But that wasn't the kicker. Intent on their perceived artistry, the stylists had mastered the art of cutting away at the air — and not the client's actual hair, which lingered between their fingers, a good two inches away from the scissors. At one point, Kim looked over at me, mentally noting that we were both getting what we would later dub "air" cuts. One of us finally said something to the stylists about not being afraid to cut off some hair. But the comment fell on deaf ears, easily drowned out by the sound of feverish, but fruitless, snipping.

Later, we hailed a cab (Kim not being the hole-in-the-ground kind a' gal at that point in time), gave the cab driver the address of *FineLine Features*, then sat back in our seats, careful to safeguard our newly-rearranged hair. It was starting to cloud up, and rain was threatening, but we were finally on our way.

We'd been to New York together a few times before (staying at my brother's and sister-in-law's) — meeting with our Casting Director, various actors, and others who would eventually become involved with our film — but we really didn't have a clue if the Bronx was up or the Battery down. So when our cab driver dropped us off, collected his fare, and drove off like a bat out of hell, we were surprised to find that we were still a full 32 blocks from our destination. The clock was ticking and neither one of us had ever won any sprinting contests. The rain was coming down now, graduating quickly from sprinkles that sweetly teased the tip of your nose to sheets of rain whipped sideways by the wind.

With practiced dexterity, Kim popped open her trusty umbrella. Not being the umbrella-popping kind a' gal (I'm from Colorado, *hello* — so is Kim, but she's also the kind that's always prepared for any eventuality), I had no umbrella to pop.

We clipped down the street, somewhere between a fast walk, a trot, and the hasty skip that comes from knowing your "air cut" is about to be assailed by a monsoon, simultaneously keeping our eyes peeled for available cabs (strangely, none appeared). I tried my best to find a place for my head under Kim's umbrella. Did I mention that we're not the same height? In fact, close to a foot separates us, which means absolutely nothing unless you're on your way to an appointment 32 blocks away with *FineLine Features*, rain is pouring down on you, and you have only the shelter of one fairly small umbrella. At that point, the foot that separates you matters.

Under normal circumstances, I really wouldn't have minded the rain. In fact, I might have welcomed it with open arms, à la Gene Kelly – heck, my firstborn daughter was named after the rain (Spring Rayne). Nor would Kim normally have minded sharing an umbrella. But, on this day, for reasons of sheer vanity, Kim and I were patently unable to appreciate nature's bounty. Kim was worried about her hair. And so was I! Not about *her* hair, of course, but about my own. Hers was naturally wavy and permanently curled, and mine was naturally curly, temporarily straightened, and both of us had just spent a lot of money to look our coiffured best.

Women will be women, and Kim wasn't happy when my attempts at sheltering my head resulted in the umbrella being moved a foot away from hers. Nor was I happy when Kim's attempts to shelter her own head resulted in my having to walk at a squat.

We battled it out covertly, but only for a short while, at which time covert fighting turned to overt fighting (not physical, of course), and Kim finally stopped dead in her tracks and exclaimed, "Couldn't you have brought your own umbrella?" Which wasn't really a question.

Kim was pissed for having to shelter the two of us when a little forethought on my part might have saved us both from the certainty of a very bad hair day and when sharing, plainly, just wasn't working. I was pissed too. Pissed that she couldn't share with a Debbie Reynolds song in her heart, regardless of the consequences. But I was also pissed for reasons beyond our mutual hair-dos, which by this time, were barely salvageable anyway. Indeed, I was pissed for the greatest, most indisputable reason of all. I was pissed *just because*. And when you're pissed *just because*, things don't always end well. And your hair gets very wet.

By the time we made it to our destination – a little late but nothing we couldn't muster up an excuse for – we had resigned ourselves to the fact that chic, good humor, and certainly our precious "air cuts" had perished under that umbrella not-made-for-two. We had to regroup – and regroup we did. Our visit with *FineLine Features* was, in the end, pleasant and entirely constructive, and our umbrella debacle quickly faded into the annals of insignificant, but ever-amusing, history.

As our story will attest to, Kim and I can go to hell and back together, but we can't share an umbrella. In fact, in all the years we've worked together, through good and bad and even downright awful, the *umbrella debacle* is the only time we've ever fought in earnest – like two hens, pecking at each other in the downpour, as if to the death, getting it over with for years to come, I guess.

I still don't carry an umbrella. Mostly because, unlike Kim, I never think of it. If I went back to New York, I might think of it, but then I might also leave the umbrella behind and just go curly.

———

In July, we heard from FineLine features.

It was nice to meet you a few weeks ago when you were in town. I apologize for taking so long to get back to you about A BUCKET OF PAINT. It's a very sweet, witty romance… Ideally, A BUCKET OF PAINT is the kind of film we would screen either in progress or finished on the festival circuit and reevaluate as an acquisition, as opposed to development project…

Likewise, October Films… found the subject matter quite delightful, and the ethnic flavor of the script to be charming… Although it didn't fit in with their current production needs, they were still encouraging… Should you produce the film independently, without a North American distributor, we would be most interested in the screening the finished film.

Encore found it to be a... *delightful story,* but they wanted *harder-edged.* Still they wanted *to consider it when completed.*

In September, Peacock proposed a distribution deal which, for myriad reasons, we weren't quite ready to consider.

1-From the 1949 film, "On the Town", screenplay by Adolph Green & Betty Comden, directed by Stanley Donen.

PING-PONG, ANYONE?
Hindsight Won't Get You a Cup of Coffee

Sept. 1995 — *We now spend a good part of our days at a large studio in the heart of Denver, but somehow, things are not feeling quite right. Kim and I sit at a couple of desks someone set up in a common area where, it seems, we can be not-so-discretely observed — or, at least, that's how it feels to us. What's going on here? If we want a private conversation, we have to get up and go find ourselves an uninhabited corner of the studio. Our files, as well, are out in the open, which bothers Kim to no end, especially since she's starting to suspect that certain people are going through them. As a defensive measure, she's started taking them home at night.*

While it's certainly exciting (the kind of excitement you feel when you see a shark fin headed your way) that things are underway, we're plagued by deeply mixed feelings (like maybe we should jump out of the water and back into the boat). Moving on to another analogy, the project is taking off at breakneck speed, and we feel like passengers on a commercial flight, gripping the arm rests, convinced that the pilot is going too fast for the runway or that we'll run out of fuel before we land. But we're the ones piloting the plane — aren't we?

Kim and I passed Ron in the hall, and he dutifully stopped to introduce us to Vance, a young man wearing a polo shirt and a pleasant expression.

"I found Vance at a coffee shop," Ron announced as if he'd brought home the new puppy. "He thought *this* sounded more interesting."

Vance shrugged his shoulders and smiled benignly.

This turned out to be the position of Production Assistant, sometimes referred to as "gopher" (go for this, go for that), a job we would have happily taken on in the years leading up to *A Bucket of Paint*. But, while we would have gladly volunteered for such a job, Vance would – per Ron's arrangement with him – be making $500 a week. Kim and I couldn't help but muse – couldn't Ron have dug up an intern? But what's done is done, and you certainly can't blame Vance for taking the money.

At least, it made sense to enlist the help of a production assistant at this point in time, as well as... well, a few other people Ron deemed indispensable at this juncture.

Or did it?

Which leads us to reflect on what was going on with Kim and me with regard to our project, control of which seemed to be slipping, slowly but ever so steadily, through our fingers. Someone once said that everything is obvious in retrospect. Unfortunately, the obvious often rises to the surface slowly, too late for the crucial moment, and then suddenly pops up in hindsight, like doughnut batter in hot oil.

In hindsight, there were several pivotal moments in what was to happen to *A Bucket of Paint*, moments that did not seem all that pivotal at the time. The first, and most obvious, of these was moving forward in any financial way when the production money itself wasn't yet in the bank.

When Ron came over to our office on Squirrel Street one day, clapped his hands together, and with great enthusiasm, said (something like) ...

"Time to get moving! It's now or never!"

... we should have unequivocally put on the brakes. Instead, we said (something like) ...

"We're still working out a couple of details on the contract. Just a few more days."

To which Ron countered (something like), "Just crossing the t's and dotting the i's, right? Come on, girls! We need to grab that studio space before someone else does!"

While it's true that the contract with our investor had been essentially ironed out, the fact that Kim and I acquiesced to Ron's entreaty, is, in retrospect, alarmingly difficult to comprehend. Our obvious reply should have been, "We're sorry, Ron. We understand how eager you are to get going. But we can only move forward in earnest when the money's made it into our account." (There was some money in our account, but it wasn't destined for this stage of the game.)

Yet, despite a vague sense of trepidation, we barely argued the point. Although it probably hadn't fully sunk in yet, we had just agreed to raise money to pay Ron and anyone else Ron planned to bring on board, not to mention studio space, to move ahead in anticipation of the big money landing in the bank in a timely fashion.

Hand-in-hand with the decision to move forward with the space, Ron urged us to sign a substantial personal guarantee to pay for lumber to start building the set or, as the argument went, lose that critical window of time. I'd never signed one before but I'm not stupid (just a little naive and overly-trusting and – okay, I'm stupid sometimes), and it was against my better judgment that I finally buckled and signed it.

So that was Pivotal Moment #1.

Which takes us back to Vance and Pivotal Moment #2.

For reasons we couldn't quite understand, despite our repeated requests, Ron had consistently neglected to provide us with one of the cell phones contracted by our company, as well as the office doors we sorely needed in order to transact the company's business with a semblance of privacy. In the face of our repeated entreaties, he also consistently failed to provide us with a key to the production offices, despite the fact that he had provided one for himself, the Production

Coordinator, the Accountant, and even, as we would later find out, a certain Production Assistant.

You know those movie scenes in which the self-effacing protagonist acts out her wildest, most empowered fantasy, kicking the antagonist's butt for all the world to see? Well, that was the fantasy. But let's be clear. Ron was not really the antagonist. In one sense, we were our own antagonists, and it was our own mutual butt we needed to kick. Though we understood what needed to happen, we were unable, for a toxic mix of reasons, to give any real weight to our words. In short, despite the tremendous headway we ourselves had already made without him, when it came to dealing with Ron, we were oddly submissive and ineffectual. So here, in retrospect, is the second fantasy. At the crucial moment, Kim and I make meaningful eye contact with each other, put on our superpower capes and say what needs to be said. After which Ron coughs up us our key, our doors, and our cell phone with a smile on his face and says, "Is there anything else I can do for you?"

But back to reality. What *had* been provided to us, oddly enough, was a ping-pong table. When we first saw it and were told it was for us (so we could unwind by playing ping-pong?), the kid in me reacted favorably. I like ping-pong! So does Kim. We immediately took up the paddles. But, soon enough, it became obvious that we were being perceived as slackers for playing. Once, in the middle of a spirited game, a voice directed at me rang out, "You need to get to work on those script changes!" As it turns out, I'd already done my script-changing duty, mainly because it was a pleasure, and not a duty to me. But here was a question. Where had the money come from to pay for the ping-pong table? Were we out raising bridge money for ping-pong paddles as well as salaries that were, at the very least, premature? We never played ping-pong again after that – well, at the studio, I mean. We couldn't play and be taken seriously, and whether anyone understood the depth of time, effort and energy that we had put into our quest to date or not, we felt we deserved to be taken seriously.

We'd also reconciled ourselves to the fact that we were paying our first production assistant $500 a week more than we were paying ourselves. But there was good news! Well, there was bad news too. The good news first. Someone had gone out and bought a fancy cappuccino-maker (at a discount, we hoped). Now the bad news. While Kim and I were scrambling to keep money in the coffers, someone had gone out and bought a fancy cappuccino-maker.

So what do you do when life hands you cappuccino-makers, discounted or not? Why, you make cappuccinos, of course! Only, we'd never made one before. We just knew a cappuccino sounded good right about now and that we needed one to ease the financial sting.

As fate would have it, Vance happened to be strolling through the main area as we were contemplating the idea. How perfect is that!

Our exchange with Vance went something like this:

"Hey, Vance! We hear there's a cappuccino-maker on the premises."

"Uh-huh."

"Would you mind terribly making us one?"

"Oh, sorry guys," Vance apologized. "Not my job."

And not quite the response we had expected.

We ended up finding some willing soul familiar with the cappuccino-maker to make us a cappuccino (thank you, willing soul), but it was not to be Vance.

Pivotal Moment #2? Yes, and here's why. What we should have said to Vance was…

"Tell you what. Why don't we talk to Ron and see if we can all get on the same page?"

Instead, one or both of us said, "Oh, okay," as Vance went on his merry way, unaware that he was leaving in his wake two bewildered, coffee-craving and subliminally pissed-off producers.

A cappuccino. Small thing. Trivial, in fact. But somehow deeply symbolic.

We acquiesced to Vance (who was just doing what he perceived to be his job, or not doing what he perceived *not* to be his job). More importantly, we failed to stand up to our Line Producer and iron out the makings of a functional working paradigm. In short, we still had not fully embraced the importance of standing up to assert ourselves as the masters and commanders of a ship we had built, plank by plank, nail by nail, with our own hands.

They say that hindsight is 20-20. If you ask me, it's 20-10. But at the end of the day, it still won't get you a cup of coffee.

MONEY, MONEY, MONEY
Scrambling to Keep Pace

Early November 1995 – *Everything is good to go with the contract – just a couple of requests we need to quickly fulfill for our investor, such as providing her with the film accountant's bio. We're almost there, and it won't be any too soon either. Up until now, it was Kim's and my business to raise money for the development of our project. Now, suddenly, we're in pre-production, raising money to pay for studio space, Ron's fees, and the fees of others coming on board at an alarming speed. We're already kicking ourselves for moving ahead prematurely. Marty, our attorney, is kicking us too, but at this point – kick as he will, and should – there's no going back. Still, all going well, that questionable decision will be a moot point, a non-issue. The money, the big money, will be in the bank. We'll be able to breathe again.*

Going into our project, Kim had excellent credit, a little money in the bank, and a respectable career that supported her creative side. So did Lauren and I – his creative side intrinsically linked, for better or worse, to mine, even to the degree that, when money was needed to keep us going during that uncomfortable period of moving forward, he bottomed out the savings ($5000) from his own hard-earned house painting money and invested it in our film. We made the decision mutually – having been together for so long, it was always a case of what's mine is ours and what's yours is ours. But no one ever worked harder for the money and parted with it so willingly. Then again, we felt pretty certain we were going to succeed in getting this film made and not just made, but made well. And, all going well, once the production money was in, he would recoup his investment, plus a little extra.

Up until now, asking others to invest in the development of our film hadn't been that difficult. In fact, it had almost been fun. Kim and I took a lot of pride in our project, in how things were developing and where they were going. Like so many "creative" people, neither one of us was, or is, a salesperson by nature, nor particularly good at the pitching process. But it's not that hard to sell something when you believe in the product. It's not that hard when you truly believe that the people you're bringing along for the journey are going to cross that finish line and be glad they signed up for the race.

Imbued with that kind of optimism and confidence, Kim and I were always able to find someone in our larger circle of friends and acquaintances, and acquaintances of acquaintances, from whom we could solicit a couple thousand dollars. My own brother, Gary, and sister-in-law, Janet, parted with $2000 each. "If things go south, I don't want you to worry about it," said my brother at the time. *Go south?* Apart from the initial cursory acknowledgment of "what-ifs", we hadn't even entertained the idea, and certainly didn't now. Didn't he know there was nothing to fear? Such was the level of our faith in our product, in ourselves, and in the future. Such was our lack of imagination. We had not yet encountered the eventually ubiquitous bumper sticker that read, *"Shit happens."* And, even if we had, we would have quickly dismissed the idea, reassuring ourselves that "shit" could never happen to us.

But now, with pressure building and monies needed for line items that should not have been coming out of development funds, raising money to see us through the week was getting a lot tougher. Migraine headaches, from which I had been a long-time sufferer, began to assault me with greater frequency. Whenever possible, I'd high-tail it to the corner store for a bag of frozen peas to apply directly to the pain or just to leave on top of my head for general relief. Without a freezer nearby, peas never stayed frozen for long, and more than once, I found myself talking on the phone while the juice of thawing peas flowed down my forehead and into my eyes. *Can you excuse me for just a quick minute? I seem to have pea juice in my eye!*

———

One question that churned in the back of our minds, only surfacing in earnest well after the fact, was *why* Ron had been so eager for us to move ahead when the production money wasn't yet in the bank and when it was in his interest to have this project go all the way to the finish line. Documented conversations of the time point to his having wanted his paychecks to start as quickly as possible. Who wouldn't? But even that doesn't really serve to explain why he would encourage a move that might very well sabotage his own long-term interests as well as our own.

We can only speculate, and one speculation we entertain is as follows. At one point, well before we had made the ill-fated decision to move ahead, Ron and Nigel had met separately with Kim. Neither I, nor Kim, remembers why I wasn't included, but it would probably be safe to say I was busy with some family-related commitment. After all, just because we were making a film, my family responsibilities weren't going away (nor would I ever have wanted them to!) At any rate, a couple of things surfaced at that meeting for which it so happened I was AWOL. First, Ron queried Kim about whether the mother of four children really had the time and energy to do this thing. "Of course," was Kim's essential reply, which was the right answer to a politically incorrect, but apparently nagging question. Secondly, Ron intimated that I (Pam) must have "money". Kim, being the soul of discretion, chose to ignore the comment. After all, my personal wealth, or lack of it, was no one else's business.

I remember laughing when Kim related the story to me. "Ron needs to come over to our house for a little visit," I suggested. "Maybe he can help me clean up the poop in the backyard." Hadn't Ron met Lauren? And hadn't Lauren been wearing his blue-collar shirt with the sewn-on name tag at the time? Did Ron really think that my seldom-changing wardrobe and Lauren's nifty name tag were some sort of well-orchestrated facade? Hadn't Ron heard the story of how Lauren had found our production investor – while painting the finder's house? If I had indeed had "money", I would long ago have gathered up all of Lauren's paint buckets and recycled them, bought him a floral swimming suit and some orange flip-flops, and sent him and the kids on a real vacation (myself included). He might still have kept his main job though, and out of gratitude if nothing else, the name tag would have remained. Or maybe it would have been framed and hung on the wall alongside the painting shirt.

No, we weren't rich, and what went into making Ron believe we were is still a puzzle to us. Whatever the case, it's conceivable that he believed moving ahead was a viable thing to do because, come what may, *money would not be an issue, even if Pam had to pull it out of her... own pocket.*

But, of course, it *was* an issue. The irony is that by agreeing to the premature start, we probably confirmed in Ron's mind what he could only (wrongly) conjecture up to that point – that money wasn't a concern.

And now, as the days and hours ticked by, bringing with them the necessity for more and more money, Kim and I were finding it hard to keep pace. But our determination not to fail before we even got started was fierce. I remember one evening in particular, holing up at our office on Squirrel Street, knowing we needed to raise $25,000 right then and there, but having no idea where to turn. Ideas were drying up, the rolodex (yes, the rolodex!) was spinning hopelessly in circles. But we weren't leaving our desks until we had a commitment. Nothing short of that would do, and before nightfall, somehow we did just that. It was a mystic feat that we would have a very difficult time repeating (yet, did repeat). For the next few days, at least, the show would go on.

We told ourselves the struggle was temporary, things never move as fast as you want them to, the real money would soon be in the bank. At this point, our Co-Producer, Gloria, was helping to raise money as well, and it helped to know there were three of us working on what was turning into a very challenging task. It certainly couldn't go on forever. But if all went well, it wouldn't have to. If we could just hold on a little longer…

Had we only understood what was going on behind the scenes with respect to Ron and his dealings with our investor! But, given our focus on raising survival money, Kim and I were quickly losing sight of the daily decisions made by Ron on behalf of our project. Who had time for minutiae, even minutiae that, in retrospect, turned out to be of fairly major importance? We were too busy scrambling up a slippery slope.

While Ron negotiated and signed deal memos, Kim and I sat outside the loop punching in phone numbers, pitching, and groveling for money to get us through the shaky interim.

By the time all was said and done, we would have raised over $300,000 to pay salaries (not for ourselves, mind you) and, well… just to keep the ball rolling.

It wasn't easy. It wasn't fun. And we still shudder when we think of it.

OUR KARMA HAS A FACE
Does Money Wear a Tight Skirt?

Mid-November 1995 *– Generally speaking and depending on the deal, investors are entitled to recoup their investment (plus some agreed-upon percentage) from first monies from the film before payment of deferred fees. But, to our surprise and chagrin, Ron has been in a back-and-forth with our investor regarding paying the actors their deferments from first monies (something he has apparently already negotiated with them), moving her to second place and putting an unexpected and serious hitch in things.*

Kim and I are (in a word) flummoxed when we find out. Ron says we will lose key actors attached to the film if we try to renegotiate terms with them. Our investor's response is very simple: first, this isn't what she bargained for, nor what the now-fleshed-out contract stipulates; secondly, all she cares about is the script and the budget, both of which suit her just fine. We love our choice of actors as much as anyone, but she has a point – not only that, she's the one with all the money. And it's kind of late in the day to be throwing a wrench into the whole works.

As we would later discover, Ron was corresponding with our attorney (Marty) regarding some critical issues without keeping us in the loop. When Marty got wind of the fact that Ron had promised to pay actors' deferments out of first monies, disregarding the original terms of our contract with our investor, he immediately sent him a memo, stating:

With respect to deferred fees, please do not promise anyone that they will be paid from 'first income from any exploitation of the film'.

Here was Ron's response:

It has always been my understanding that deferments are considered a part of the cost of the negative, and must be paid from first money, prior to recoupment, profit participation etc. I have already told this to several cast and crew members whom I have asked to take deferments. I myself have a substantial deferment. If we are now going to ask these people to take a longer wait for payment, I think we will be in trouble...

By this time, it was apparent to all – our investor and ourselves included – that Ron was running the show. After all, he was the one making deals – in this case, attempting to re-negotiate the most critical deal of all. I'm not sure where that put Kim and me in the eyes of cast and crew, but I suspect "subordinate to Ron" might put it gently. Granted, we had early on made the decision to hand him the reins of the project, but reporting to us was an essential step in the process, since the legal responsibilities of the project fell on us no matter how peripherally Ron might view our importance.

Maybe because we never had the right "fit" to begin with, or maybe because we failed to tailor the fit when the shoe started hurting, the line between Ron, and Kim and I, quickly became blurred. When the fog finally lifted, Ron could be seen sitting behind his desk in front of a large, flowing banner mounted on the wall (someone's gift to him) that read, "Congratulations, Cecil B. DeLong!" (a reference to Cecil B. DeMille, one of the most successful filmmakers and producers of all time). We weren't sure exactly what that said about the situation, but in some otherwise inexpressible and deeply ironic way, the banner seemed to say it all.

Kim and I still believed in Ron's overall abilities, even if, for reasons unknown, he wasn't really keeping us informed or replying to our requests. Still, if he could just help us get to the finish line now – utilizing production experience that we felt was crucial at this point –

we could live with the recurring, sometimes overwhelming, frustrations.

I'd like to stop right here and say that a pet peeve of mine is the perception of certain people (usually not-so-nice ones) that niceness is a sure sign of weakness. Let's face it – it takes a lot of guts to remain nice, both at heart and in terms of one's behavior, in the face of a sometimes mean and manipulative world. And, despite the perception of some, I've never thought of Kim, or myself, as weak – either then, or now. However, I do have to say, methinks we were pretty damn dumb!

Let me elaborate. While, admittedly, we were guilty of some dumb moves in the standard sense of the word (i.e., lacking in sense) – what I really mean here is *dumb* in the sense of being *unable to speak*, or *refraining from speaking*. In short, somewhere along the way, Kim and I had been struck dumb.

Make no mistake. There is an expiration date on the speaking-up window of opportunity, and ours was fast approaching.

―――

Ron was on the phone with our investor, hashing things out (exactly how and when had he become the project's spokesperson with our investor, even retrospect has not clarified) when Candi first wobbled through the studio door. She came to us courtesy of Gloria who, if we remember correctly, had met her by way of a mutual affiliation with a certain banking institution. I don't think Gloria really *knew* Candi – anymore than you might know anyone in passing – but somewhere in the conversation, Candi picked up that we were in the middle of a multi-million-dollar feature film project that was experiencing some financial difficulties. Her curiosity peaked, Candi decided to pay the studio a visit.

The truth was that we urgently needed $500,000 in bridge money. *Why was that much bridge money needed?* you ask. Well, essentially because the "deferment issue" with our investor was causing grave delays in the money being delivered. Delays quickly become dollar signs (people and studio time still have to be paid), inflating the original budget with the speed of a prairie fire. Meantime, Kim and I were left to scramble to raise more interim money, but by this time, our money-raising threshold had pretty much been reached.

Gloria introduced us to Candi. Candi shook our hands, her inordinately long, but artfully decorated, fingernails digging deeply into our flesh (an omen of things to come?).

What is it they say about first impressions? Trust them? Don't trust them? Listen to your gut? Don't listen to your gut? They say a lot of purportedly wise things, I guess, but the upshot is, a first impression can be either deeply revealing or shockingly misleading, depending on a lot of things, the life conditions of those involved, the barometric pressure, and the alignment of the planets included.

In a word, our first impression of Candi (speaking for both Kim and me, as our mental notes on the subject concur): *Huh?* Candi was pretty in a way that is difficult to define. Let me try. You knew there was beauty there or that there had been – you just couldn't quite tell where it was coming from under the layers of general chaos. But even that doesn't quite capture her puppy dog essence that pulled at your heartstrings even as she (figuratively, of course) pissed all over your brand new carpet.

Men were unabashedly attracted to her and, in fact, even the wisest of them seemed to leave his faculties behind in the face of her odd, wounded-bird vulnerability.

It was difficult to tell, at least in that first conversation, where Candi's head was really "at" because, as we would later come to suspect but were never in a position to confirm, any inherent coherence she possessed seemed to be held captive by a drug habit, the full extent of which – prescription, maybe? – we never quite grasped. On a good day, she could hold her own in a conversation –

on a bad one, you hadn't the foggiest idea what she was talking about. And yet, her sincerity almost always overwhelmed you, to the degree that you hated yourself for ever questioning her ability to do just what she insisted she could do – over and over again and in the most creative and outlandish ways. Come up with the cash.

In retrospect (ah, good old retrospect! – one day I will write a poem in your honor), if our guts and/or our minds were perplexed by the enigma that was Candi, there was one huge tip-off we made note of, but chose – like anyone who ever preferred faint hope to stark reality – to ignore.

There seemed to be nothing real about her. Now, I have nothing in the least against self-improvement through surgery, not to mention the even less invasive techniques available today (which weren't quite so available back then). It could even be convincingly argued that I could use a few. And, in fact, maybe someday I'll happily join the club. Come to think of it, I have an appointment next Friday (I don't, but maybe by the time you're reading this, I will). But it wasn't just the look of Candi, which seemed to lack a healthy glow despite the alterations – it was the overall, pervasive artifice. Even her voice rang false, as if she'd borrowed it to fit today's persona, begging the obvious question – *Who is she, really?*

As if to underscore the flagrant deceit, she wore stiletto heels and a short, skin-tight skirt and tottered not-so-gracefully across the cement floor, making me think of… well, how I might perform under similar circumstances, having never worn stilettos in my life. We were deeply grateful she didn't break an ankle on the premises.

But here's the question. Does money have a look? a walk? a voice? Does it wear a tight skirt? Does it wear bad hair extensions? It takes all kinds to make a world and, surely, money makes its way into the hands of all kinds of people. So, how, in the end, do you gauge the value, or the reality, of a person's bank account or ability to secure large sums of money?

Well, first you and your attorney do due diligence to validate the individual's authenticity. After all, anyone can walk in your door. And anyone can tell you, without batting a fake eyelash, that they can not only come up with $500,000, but with a whopping $5,000,000.

THINGS GET UGLY
New Outfits and an Empty Bank Account

Nov. 10th 1995 – *Candi has delivered a letter of intent, signed by one of the most prominent and well-to-do commercial real estate investors in Denver, with whom she is apparently affiliated and through whom she intends to finance the entire film. Of course, this would mean blowing off our original investor, something Kim and I are very reluctant to do. In fact, the idea is repugnant to us from two perspectives – one, a bird in the hand is worth two in the bush -- and more importantly – switching from a bona-fide investor who's been supportive of our project and of us as women in the industry, to someone with whom we have no history or allegiance, goes against our grain and our remaining common sense. However, Ron reiterates in no uncertain terms that she (our original investor) will not commit to additional funds (now needed as a result of delays), nor will she go ahead with funding when the original terms and conditions of our contract have been contradicted (via deal memos in which actors and others – instead of her – are promised first monies).*

Feeling as if our backs were against the wall, Kim and I finally agreed with Ron that there was no other clear option at this point but to "go with Candi". Bad decision. It should be emphasized, however, that we alone were to blame for not keeping better tabs on the direction Ron was taking on our behalf, for allowing him to continue to deal with our investor and, ultimately, for making decisions, however convincing the argument, that ran against our better judgment. There was no denying it – either then or now – at the end of the day, the fault was ours, not his, and no one else's. That said, let's move on.

Before committing to Candi, we called Marty (our attorney) to talk with him about the situation, faxed him the letter of intent, and brought him to Denver to meet Candi in person. For better or worse (worse) she and her lender passed the due diligence test. In fact, it turned out that Candi had been successfully involved with a long list of high-stake business ventures, including one acquisition between two Fortune 100 companies to the tune of $485 million. On one hand, given her general bearing, this was hard to believe. On the other hand, those seemed to be the facts.

Later in the month, Joan (our original investor) would indicate in writing that she was willing to consider (given adherence to the original terms of the contract) funding in conjunction with the new investor who, in this scenario, would provide the additional monies needed as a result of delays and added production costs, but – she stipulated – at this point, we would have to re-apply for funding. Kim and I were keenly aware that this would take a hopelessly (in the context of our situation) long time. Nor was there any guarantee, as our investor made clear, that we would be able to secure approval this time around. And then, there was still the deferment issue. The option did exist to bring everything to a grinding halt and pursue the possibility she put forward, but at this point, we were already in too deep in terms of monies owed. In a Nov. 14th memo to us from Ron regarding short-term financial needs, our obligation to make the upcoming payroll was spelled out, as well as a litany of other needs, including an obligation to make a substantial deposit to SAG (the Screen Actors Guild) if we wanted the actors available to start filming as scheduled, on the 29th of November.

The problem was, as an escalating budget flashed before our eyes, we and others involved were in a big, fat hurry to get that financial infusion. What Kim and I hadn't yet learned and embraced was that a big, fat hurry seldom serves anyone. In fact, it could be argued that there's nothing more dangerous than being in a big, fat hurry. More often than not, haste really does make waste and – efficiently-utilized – time is the deceptively nonchalant friend who's really on your side.

And so it was that we made the switch to a new investor. We signed the formal investor agreement with Candi on Nov. 14th, with monies promised immediately... which was none too early, given the fact that a majority of our principal actors had arrived in Denver on Nov. 13th for rehearsals.

———

Before the switch had hit the fan, we had planned a "welcome" dinner with the actors at a nice Denver restaurant known in particular for its great seafood, and were now trying desperately to drag our appetites along with us – not an easy task, given the circumstances of the last week and the lack of money in the bank. Still, it was a lovely affair, one we had looked forward to and now managed to cherish and enjoy, even if we didn't dine with quite as much gusto as we might have. Gloria paid for the dinner as part of her investment and personally paid for a beautiful pair of earrings for Kim and a new outfit for me, so that we could look our best (in my case, maybe a little hipper) for the occasion.

Due in large part to financial matters that were newly weighing on our minds, Kim and I have only a hazy remembrance of what should have been a memorable evening. In trying to reconstruct the event, we think we remember Nigel, Ron, Charles Durning, Jim True, Mare Winningham, and Julie Hagerty. However, our memory is based on airline logs and not on working brain cells. We do know that Jim True was there, as I sat next to him, and that Charles Durning was there, as Kim sat next to him. And we vaguely remember exchanging personal and professional stories, laughing, and generally doing our best to celebrate an event that had already lost most of its celebratory appeal, at least to Kim and me and I'm sure, to some degree, Gloria.

I also remember that, while my clothes may have looked hip, I felt about as hip as… what's the expression? … a broken hip.

Rehearsals were scheduled to begin the next day at the Helix, a nice downtown Denver hotel which enjoyed a reputation for catering to movie stars and other celebrity types. With the ticking of every consecutive minute, Kim and I became more anxious for the promised money to come in and less able to simply enjoy what should have been a joyous time for us. Payroll was coming due, and how were we going to meet that deadline if Candi didn't come through in a timely fashion?

Things were tense, to say the least.

While Kim did her best to take care of things on the money front, i.e., put out as many fires as she could, I attended rehearsals, at least in part to maintain a semblance of normalcy. *Normalcy* was about the last thing I was feeling in the pit of my stomach.

Sitting in a quiet corner with Nigel, Mare Winningham and Charles Durning, discussing rehearsal details, I happened to look down at my left foot, where my heel was jutting slightly from my slip-on shoe. Exposed for everyone to see (though if anyone did see it, they courteously pretended not to) was a big hole inside the heel of my shoe, which I had tried to cover, for reasons unknown to me now, with a generous wad of toilet paper. As unobtrusively as possible, I slid my heel back into my shoe, not unaware of the symbolism. One of those moments you know you'll laugh about someday, while completely unable to laugh about it at the moment. (Dress me up in the hippest clothes, you'll still find a hole in my shoe, leaving no doubt as to my lifetime membership in the rank and file.)

Once rehearsals started, I found myself able, at least here and there, to leave my worries behind. It was such fun (albeit, restrained fun) to watch things unfold! At one point, I was asked to stand in for Julie who was back in California until the next day, in a scene that called for me to give Charles Durning a kiss on the cheek. My acting skills were nothing to brag about, but the kiss I gave him was heartfelt. He seemed to be such a dear man, and had been (and would continue to be) very kind to us.

There was another distraction for me to enjoy, and that was Drake Bell, the young actor who would be playing nine-year-old "Teebs". His disposition was nothing short of sunny, and as I hung out with him in the downstairs lobby of the hotel, he filled me in on the magic tricks he was practicing in his spare time. Since there were no dogs roaming around the hotel to fill my aching soul, young Drake Bell's energy would have to do.

One thing we were not looking forward to was Candi visiting rehearsals. She had expressed an interest in doing so and, certainly, as the new Executive Producer (who hadn't quite yet produced the money), she deserved (or did she?) the opportunity to meet the actors, if that was her desire. Kim's and my concern centered around two things: 1) Candi could never get the actors' names straight – Charles Durning was always Charles Durling, and you couldn't tell her otherwise; and, 2) she might take the opportunity to finally fall on her face in those stiletto heels and land on someone critical to the completion of the film. (That may sound like a bit of sarcasm, but believe me, it's not. Well, okay, maybe it is, but as someone who tends to trip over her own two feet at the least propitious moments, I am painfully aware of the possibilities.)

I can't speak for the actors' reactions to her when she finally did make her advent. She was bubbly and effusive enough, though how much of that was pharmaceutically-generated was anyone's guess. Nor did she fall on her face for anyone to see. So, we were grateful for that. But, plainly speaking, Kim and I were on pins and needles until the arranged meeting had come to a blessed end. I imagine there were raised eyebrows, and perhaps even some shared bewilderment, but in the end, the actors may simply have told themselves what we did. You can't judge a book by its cover, or by the way the author pronounces your last name.

On top of everything else, we had something else to worry about. The production company had apparently rented a fancy Cadillac in which to ferry Charles Durning around. *A Cadillac?* (What we really needed here was my Mom supervising the budget.) But the cost of renting a Cadillac wasn't what I was most worried about – it was the still-teenaged driver, my daughter, Dawn (whose big idea was that?), who, at the time, had a habit of driving like a bat out of hell. (*Speeding Ticket* was her middle name, though she's since had it changed to *Drives Like a Mommy*.) Somehow they both survived the experience, and Charles Durning (even as he must have held on to his arm rest for dear life) was so sweet to Dawn that his kindness has never been forgotten by either Dawn or me. In an effort to encourage her growth and awareness of the world, he even gave her a handwritten list of his favorite books to read.

Hours ticked by loudly, money was still not in the bank, and things were coming to a head. Tensions were running high, and the animosity toward Kim and me, which would eventually build to an almost unbearable crescendo, was beginning to show its hostile face.

Paige, an acting coach and sympathetic woman who was one of our development investors, was privy one day to the ugliness that was beginning to bleed through the project's pores. "Why can't everyone just get together and share a pot of baked beans?" she ruminated out loud.

It's an image that has always stuck with me. People united, working with a joyful attitude toward the common goal – over a pot of baked beans. It was too much to expect – that I understand. But in a better world, on another planet, creative ideas might have come from it. Collaboration. Synergy. It might have been the attitude that turned the tide for *A Bucket of Paint*. To this day, when someone bemoans the fate of the world and wonders why we can't all just get along... I want to say with all sincerity, "Yeah, over a pot of baked beans!"

Candi was clearly running late on her delivery of the production money, but she assured us that the delay would be short-lived. That being the case, Paige made the decision to up her investment and come through with the payroll. We accepted, with both gratitude and discomfort. The whole thing was beginning to feel like the kind of slippery slope that could potentially herald a landslide. Yet, we had no choice but to banish the thought and keep on going.

Ever notice how painstaking and time-consuming it is to build anything worthwhile – yet how quickly that very thing can start to crumble? Within days, Kim and I felt compelled to make everyone aware of the precarious situation in which we now found ourselves. Our Co-Producer, Gloria, expressed her desire to speak with the construction crew regarding our lack of liquidity. We then followed up with our own crew meeting, in which we answered questions as best we could. There wasn't much to say, except that we were still hopeful. Most of the crew just stood there, expressionless. It was painful all around and certainly did nothing to add to our popularity.

The next hurdle was talking to actors and some of the department heads. This meeting took place at the Helix Hotel, site of our rehearsals. Before going in, I took a moment to plunge my nose into an enormous flower arrangement that graced the lobby, boasting lilies and a great profusion of color. As if to infuse my life with all that flowers represent for me – hope, rebirth, beauty – did I say *hope*? – I inhaled deeply, then broke away, only to find my nose itching and my fingers laden with a thick yellow pollen. I hastened to the bathroom, where I discovered my entire nose and surrounding area covered in yellow. I wiped, I washed, I wiped again. But I couldn't escape my newly jaundiced appearance. So be it. Maybe the new look would elicit pity.

I walked into the room and took a seat at a large conference table where others had already gathered. For arbitrary reasons, Kim and I had decided I would do the talking. I did my best, expressing that the project had had so much support in the past that I couldn't see things folding now. And that was true. But I had no substance on which to rest that faith, other than my faith in life itself.

Everyone seemed to listen, and I really appreciated that no one chose the moment to grill or condemn us. In fact, someone – I wish I could remember who – came up behind me as I was talking and squeezed my shoulder in a rare show of empathy, if not actual support. It was as close to baked beans as we would ever come.

A BUCKET OF PAIN
The Case of the Fleeing Intern

November 1995 *– We still don't have the money, but by gosh, Candi and her ever-changing assortment of funding sources (whatever happened to her original funding source?) assure us that those "codes" are coming, and if we'll just sit by the fax machine, we're bound to see them arrive. We're still hopeful, but we can't deny that it's starting to look pretty bad. Still, we can't, and won't, abandon ship, though it's becoming pretty apparent that we've sideswiped an iceberg. The scene is starting to get uglier, yet we feel we have no choice but to ride it out and pray for the best.*

Jagan was an intern who boarded the ship some days prior to impact with the iceberg. Though he had expressed a certain interest in feature film making, he was a neuroscientist at heart and in practice who had come to us via one of our development investors. Jagan was one of the good guys, kind and easy-going, and we were happy to have him.

We installed a desk for him in one of the offices adjoining the main area where he could freely move about and observe the goings-on. Above his door was a sign that read, *A Bucket of Paint*. I don't remember if there were similar signs above other office doors – there was no question that this was the general *A Bucket of Paint* domain – but perhaps Jagan was especially proud of his affiliation with the project. Either that or someone had just taped the sign there in case the neuroscientist lost his way.

In any event, Jagan had probably just started to get comfortable with the daily grind when the project began taking a turn. The shift in atmosphere was palpable, and I think, at first, Jagan was intrigued by the plot twist in an otherwise mundane story. Finally, he'd have something interesting (though potentially depressing) to report! He tuned in and even joined the daily, early-morning floggings – as a bystander, mind you, not as a flogger. It must be emphasized that Jagan didn't seem to have an unkind bone in his body. He was merely a (somewhat) impartial observer, taking mental notes until the emotional burden became too heavy to bear.

It's interesting how – perhaps as a mental shortcut – your mind will create a picture by which to recall certain life-moments. Kim and I remember those daily meetings as floggings, but alternately, we remember them as tomato-throwing affairs, or inquisitions akin to… you know, that Spanish one. The multitude of arms crossed in front of the multitude of chests, the many sets of eyes piercing our own… and then the final test: would Kim and I float in the water, thereby confirming our guilt, or would we sink and drown, thereby proving our innocence?

In the years since, we've read about other producers whose ships went down, whether by loss of funding or through some other mishap or misstep, who didn't seem to experience the enduring angst that was the hallmark of our ailing production. Why we (and perhaps as a consequence, others) handled things differently is a thought-provoking question, the answers to which aren't all negative. Kim and I were (and are) by nature honest, optimistic and conscientious. We were genuine die-hards, devoted to the project and reluctant to let it go. We were also new to the process, naïve, and perhaps a bit too eager to believe that our index fingers plugged into the ship's massive wounds would do the trick. In fact, we were extremely hesitant to remove our fingers, though it could be argued that removing them swiftly might have been the merciful thing to do for all concerned, ourselves included.

But back to Jagan…

One day, as a particularly ripe tomato was being flung in my direction, my eyes reflexively caught his, and I found myself wondering how he was reacting to what he was witnessing. To add to the mayhem, the construction workers had taken to revving up their chain saws on the set of the beautiful $200,000 Victorian they had been constructing. Easily audible through the heating ducts, this was meant as a threat to the existing construction and, by extension, to our production. The noise was earsplitting, but more than that, it was unnerving. Of course, that was the point.

To the gentle of heart, these meetings that seemed to ooze of mob-mentality couldn't possibly have been a pretty scene and, indeed, there sat Jagan, huddled within the circle of accusation, the look of shock on his face so manifest that my empathy toward him exceeded my own self-pity. He looked downright stupefied.

Meantime, the questions kept coming. They came in different shapes and forms, but only at one level of intensity (intense). Essentially they boiled down to this:

Where's the money? and (maybe more importantly) *When are we getting paid?*

Perhaps as a self-defense mechanism, I found myself tuning out the noise, the barrage of questions, and became, like Jagan, something of an impartial observer. *So this is human nature! Interesting. Oh look, there's the spokesperson for the construction workers! He must be stressed out because the Assistant Production Coordinator is giving him a shoulder massage. Wait – I think he's saying something. Maybe I should tune in. Something about the fact that Kim and I should never have tried to make a movie in the first place. Okay. And something about going to the Labor Board. I hope Kim's tuning in because I think I'm going to tune out again.*

Somewhere along the line, Ron had jumped the fence and was now standing squarely on the side of our interrogators. No longer presenting himself as captain of the ship, he was simply someone vying for a lifeboat – at least for now.

Just to the side of the circle of accusation, calmly knitting, sat a visitor to the set who, though not part of the filmmaking team, happened to have a stake in how things were unfolding. Though it wasn't her intent to be, or to come across as, anything but unobtrusive, given my own state of mind, I couldn't help but flash on the tricoteuses (knitting women) of the French Revolution, who sat beside the guillotine, knitting away, during Paris's public executions. That's just where my own head was "at", no double entendre intended.

The flogging went on, the tomatoes flew, the inquisition roared, the knitting needles clashed, and then, once again, it was over, to be continued the next day. In mutual disgust and anger, the interrogators got up. Ron and other crew members went one way, while Kim and I headed toward the dugout where we were holed up, still trying to keep things alive.

Some minutes before the meeting's end, Jagan had suddenly got up and left the circle. Kim and I vaguely noted it, but didn't think much of it, other than to be glad, for his sake, that he wasn't sticking around. It wasn't until later, when we wondered how he was faring and went looking for him, that we realized he had flown the coop. As a parting gesture, or perhaps as a coded message and expression of his deepest feelings, he had torn the "t" off his sign, leaving it to read *A Bucket of Pain*.

We never saw him again.

BATHTUB BLUES
A Heart for Any Fate

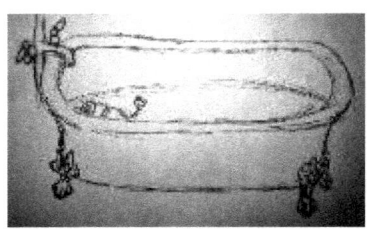

November 1995 *— In the words of Yogi Berra, it's déja-vu all over again — a replay of funds not coming in. Things are getting worse — if for no other reason than because they're not getting any better. But bad is bad, tough is tough — nuances don't really make a difference — and still, there is no light at the end of the tunnel.*

In the middle of all this, my good friend Sue, from Illinois, has arrived, massage chair in tow, to offer free chair massage to anyone who needs the knots worked out. The original idea, conceived when things were at their happiest and most hopeful, was to create a relaxed and healthful atmosphere on the set, to add to the peace and serenity that were supposed to prevail. Now Sue's mission is uncertain. It's clear we all need a massage — both external and internal — but the overall mood at the studio isn't lending itself to the receptivity originally hoped for. A few souls are able to let down their guard in deference to their tense and aching muscles, and that would definitely include me, a big believer in massage therapy. But poor Sue! She's a trooper, no doubt, but I'm sure this isn't exactly what she envisioned when she got off the plane.

Sometimes you can only do so much. And then, content in the knowledge that you gave it your best shot, you just have to get back on the plane and go home again.

I've always been a morning person. This propensity for early-morning rising was, at least to some degree, ingrained in me by my mother, who – in an effort to infuse me with a zest for living equal to her own, and later, in her single-minded quest for a tennis opponent – liked to jolt me out of bed on Saturday mornings, all the while lustily reciting from Longfellow's, "A Psalm of Life":

> *Let us then be up and doing,*
> *With a heart for any fate;*
> *Still achieving, still pursuing,*
> *Learn to labor and to wait!*

(The exclamation point at the end of that stanza is mine, put there to capture my mother's enthusiasm.)

After which, I would, without protest, get up and put on my little tennis skirt, showing off my still-young legs. And then, despite my vain-glorious attempts at perfect form, the little tennis dynamo with the wackiest serve on the planet would proceed to whip my ass.

But I digress.

Even after *A Bucket of Paint* took its fateful turn, I was still a morning person (in addition to being a mourning person…). Nothing too surprising there. What was difficult to explain to myself was why I was suddenly sleeping better than I ever had in my life. Tossing and turning had always been a nightly ritual. I wouldn't label it insomnia, exactly, just me taking advantage of the quiet time to mentally resolve the world's problems. Now, suddenly, I knew what it was like to be my brother Johnny, who (as a kid) would fall asleep the second his head hit the pillow. I knew what it was to sleep through the night and wake up – dare I say it? – refreshed.

They say that those who sleep well at night aren't troubled by guilty consciences. But I did have a guilty conscience – a guilty conscience about the fact that I was actually sleeping well. Shouldn't I have been pacing the floor at night, pulling my hair out, gnashing my teeth – at the least, not sleeping? I'm sure there are those who felt it was the least I should suffer. Maybe sleep was a refuge for me. Maybe I went to it every night in anticipation of sweet forgetfulness, like a babe to its mother's arms. Maybe I was just downright exhausted after yet another punishing day. Whatever the case, I was extremely grateful for the benefit of sleep. I needed it desperately, and quite fortunately, I got it.

At the end of those grueling days, after I would finally get home at night, after dinner, after evening prayers with my husband (strength! wisdom! resolution!), I would run myself a bath and slowly sink into the hot water. There's no better stress-reliever than a nice hot bath, but it's also the perfect place to cry – a feeling I would later describe this way in a work of fiction: "…as she splashed water over her face, there was no telling where the bathwater ended and where her personal grief began."

One evening, as I was running yet more hot water into the tub, my daughter, Dawn, came into the bathroom and took a seat. Growing up, my kids always felt at liberty to disturb my bathing bliss to discuss the smallest thing – what was for dinner, their need for a new backpack, the fact that it was raining. Whatever. Three seconds past the age of five – they, however, would have been totally mortified had I barged in on them, even to tell them the house was on fire. At any rate, many of our most meaningful dialogues were carried out in that way – me bathing, they not caring one iota that I was stark naked under my lavender bubbles. I was "Mom", after all, and modesty wasn't really relevant. Yes, yes, I know. I could have used the opportunity to teach them a thing or two about respectful modesty. But the truth was – much in the same way that America apparently enjoyed FDR's fireside chats in the 50s– I enjoyed those little bathroom chats with my kids.

So Dawn walked in on me. I wasn't overly self-conscious at the tell-tale signs of crying on my face, as Dawn had had occasion to be with me at the studio, a quiet witness to much of what was going down – unlike my husband who had never visited the set, at first because it was hard to find the right moment, and now, because the last thing I wanted was for him to witness how ugly things had gotten for us. At any rate, Kim and I had initially brought Dawn on board (as an unpaid production assistant) to experience the creation of something beautiful, but here we were going down the tubes, and I recalibrated my brain to view the event as a needed lesson in her young life (as well as an apparently needed lesson in my own middle-aged life). Take note of how people behave in a crisis, I thought to myself. And watch us. Kim and I may not be winning this one, but if we have to go down, we'll do it with our humanity intact. Despite my tears – maybe half a bathtub full – this was my inner pledge.

"Don't worry, Mom," she said, taking a seat on the floor. "It's gonna be okay."

"I know, honey," I said.

"If we lose the house, we'll just go up to the mountains."

"Sounds good to me." The mountains had always been a sanctuary for me, a source of strength reminding me that my troubles were insignificant when measured against their majesty.

"We could build a cabin." She sounded strangely excited about the possibility.

And, strangely, the thought of us up in the mountains, chopping trees, fending off bears, building a little log cabin together, was cheering to me as well.

"We could," I said.

From Kim:

The simple truth is we went into this project with an open heart, to create a great experience for everyone, with the hope of making money for everyone. The fact that we wound up hurting people – that was just unfathomable. The worst kind of pain we experienced was the knowledge that we had caused others pain.

I had never gone through anything quite like this, where my integrity was being attacked at every corner and we were being shredded apart by people who truly knew nothing about us. I guess I learned to take refuge in a kind of numbness of spirit. Let me tell you, being numb has its advantages!

That being said, Pam and I were the Producers, so no matter what, we always knew it was our duty to keep it going. There was no question in my mind about that. We were responsible – we had to take responsibility. Perhaps my many years as a paralegal helped me through, as my job was often stressful due to time constraints and I had to deal with many personalities... occasionally, some not so pleasant. Still, I'd never experienced anything quite like this. I managed to keep my composure – yet, nothing stopped my stomach from churning or my neck from being in a constant knot.

There was also something disconcerting about observing people fall apart and get so nasty. Although I could sometimes separate myself from the ugliness of it all, it was still mind-boggling to see the change in some of these people – people who, at one time, had been cheerful and approachable. I felt like an outcast, unable to solicit a smile from once-friendly people, walking around the set in a diseased state for which the only cure was money... and lots of it!

Processing the chaos, as well as the agony of the unknown, kept me so busy I had a hard time thinking straight. I couldn't fathom what was happening to us. It was simply unthinkable that we were headed for disaster.

At the worst moments, I reminded myself of what was important in life, something that was brought home to me through the painful experience of losing both my father and my brother at a young age. And I knew that, as bad as things were now, they didn't represent the worst. My family was a source of support, but I lived alone and didn't have the comfort of someone's arms to run to at night. I did talk frequently with my best friend from childhood, Anna, who offered both a shoulder to lean on and a needed ear. Yet, as helpful as that was, only Pam and I could really understand what the other was going through from day to day. After all, we were living it – surviving it – together.

What did I do to keep sane on the worst of nights? Ironically, I curled up and watched a movie.

A GRINDING HALT
The Long Bridge to Nowhere

Mid-November 1995 – *A publicist and still photographer[1] have been retained, which feels a little ironic, given our tenuous circumstance and the sea of unsmiling photographic subjects. An announcement appears in the entertainment column of a major Denver newspaper, heralding the filming of A Bucket of Paint. Is this denial on our end, or just the irony of bad timing?*

Action!

Rehearsals have started for a movie to be shot in Denver after Thanksgiving.

The feature's a romantic comedy called ▮▮▮▮▮ and stars **Charles Durning, Cyd Charisse, Mare Winningham** and **Julie Haggerty**. The director's **Nigel Nobel**, the guy who made the stunning documentary *Voices of Sarafina*. And the screenplay is by local writer **Pamela Nelson**.

The story concerns a traditional Irish-American family headed by Durning. Things get dicey when a non-Irish guy falls for one of Durning's two daughters.

Bit parts have been cast — but lotsa locals will be used as extras. Watch this space for info.

Charles Durning

```
You could "watch this space for info" 'til your face turned
   blue, but this was going to be the last mention of it.
(The "non-Irish guy" part wasn't accurate, nor was the spelling of
  Julie's or Nigel's last names, but it was still publicity, for
         which we normally would have been grateful.)
```

My parents, whom I have never kept in the loop (first, I wanted to surprise them, then I wanted to spare them) take stock of the newspaper column over scrambled eggs and call me up. They don't say it, but I can tell they're proud. Mom always loved Cyd Charisse. I thank them for their enthusiasm and good wishes, but secretly wish they'd skipped reading the newspaper that morning and gone straight to watching the History Channel.

There seemed to be no way to staunch the bleeding. Candi's promises simply weren't giving rise to money, and now she was in serious default. The result was – according to our accountant's estimates (via Ron) – a need for about $500,000 in bridge money, a figure which would grow with every passing day spent in default.

But there was hope on the horizon! A wealthy couple was coming in to check out the set, speak with us and Candi personally, and decide whether it made good business sense to write a check. Let me stop right there and say that investing in a movie is seldom equated with good business sense. As our investment contracts made a point of spelling out, film is risky business. That doesn't mean that people don't sometimes get rich investing in film – it's just that they get rich in the same way they might hit it big in Vegas – playing as wisely as possible, but still relying on lady luck at the end of the day.

But, if you have the money to gamble, you're willing to take a chance, and you think you might just have a shot at a winner, why the heck not? This was apparently the case with Madeline and Grant.

We made arrangements for them to visit the set after hours, and made sure Candi would be there to meet with them. After all, the $500,000 would be a bridge to her promised multi-million-dollar production money. They needed to know that her side of the deal was, for lack of better words, *real*.

Kim and I had extremely mixed feelings at this point about raising bridge money, as there was certainly the chance of it being a bridge to nowhere. But Candi was still so adamant about the fact that the money was coming in, and debts were piling so high in the interim, that we felt we had to go for it. It should also be noted that Candi wasn't hiding her face, though sometimes we wished she would, simply because she had yet to bring us any good news. In this case, no news was bad news, and the bad news was getting pretty hard to take. And, yet, Candi (and, by now, her nice and apparently stable boyfriend, Jack) were a fairly consistent presence, giving some weight to her sincerity and faith in her own rhetoric, if nothing else. If she was just a flake, or a fraud, or an evil prankster, we asked ourselves, why hadn't she by now disappeared into the mist into which all villains eventually vanish?

Kim and I had one big concern, however, and shared it with Candi well before the meeting.

"Why don't you let us do most of the talking?" I suggested, not because I was worried about anything but the truth coming out, but because Candi sometimes lacked coherence. We even found a way to suggest she stay "clean" for the occasion – well, maybe the words we chose weren't quite so… on-the-nose, given the fact that neither we, nor she, spoke openly about her suspected, but still hypothetical, use of drugs. We simply asked her to be at her *best*, a euphemism for *please watch what you put in your mouth or up your nose*.

"Whatever questions they might have," I went on, "just answer honestly. And try not to get off track." That we were dictating comportment to our Executive Producer might seem completely out of line, but in this case, there were no holds barred, even if our attitude smacked of condescension. Because, yes, there was condescension on our part – but there was also a demonstration of patience, tolerance, and compassion toward her that was way above and beyond the call of duty, given the fact that her stringing us along and failing to deliver were having an impact, not just on the project, but on the fabric of our lives and the lives of so many others.

Candi nodded. She seemed to get it.

"Just relax and be calm," Kim added. "And don't leave the room until the meeting's over, okay?" She had a habit of sneaking away at odd moments to places unknown to do who knows what.

Before joining us for the meeting, Madeline and her husband toured the set. They were impressed (the Victorian house was still standing and, quite frankly, it *was* impressive.). Somewhere in the course of the evening, we were informed that Madeline might be ready and able to write a check that night. But right now she was going to meet with us and Candi. Apparently, the decision to invest or not was going to be hers, and she would meet with us alone. Or maybe she felt her fact-finding mission in all-woman territory would be more effective without her husband in tow.

Madeline was a well-to-do, well-dressed, well-put-together woman who exuded intuitive good sense that bordered on x-ray vision. She was smart and friendly, and we liked her instantly.

Candi seemed clear-headed, just this side of charming. In short, and as requested, at her *best*. She smiled, spoke in short sentences, and deferred to us whenever appropriate. In fact, the meeting seemed to be going extremely well, and Madeline gave the impression of being comfortable in our midst.

Then, the fateful moment came. Candi suddenly excused herself from the room.

Kim and I looked at each other. *Oh no!* We hastily turned to Madeline to resume the conversation, hoping against hope that our worst nightmare would not materialize. In short order, Candi returned to the room, and the nightmare quickly began. From all appearances, she was high as a kite and not afraid to fly.

The visual that remains in our brains about what ensued is of two women facing each other, their long, polished fingernails doing a fingernail duet. It was sophisticated fingernail sign language, and — like two captives in an alien spaceship – Kim and I could only watch and wonder at the spectacle before us. Candi's nails played, pointed, encircled, even managed to giggle and cajole. Madeline's nails were equally lively, but slightly less spontaneous and more calculated – maybe because they were busy carrying out an undercover investigation.

Despite the fact that Candi was making very little sense (at least, to Kim and me), the two women seemed to be getting along famously. Still, there was no doubt that Madeline had the upper hand (so to speak).

Finally, the meeting ended, and Madeline said her pleasant goodbyes. We looked at Candi the way you might an errant child. There was really nothing left to say. No reason to be angry. Well, lots of reasons, none of which would get us any closer to the money.

Later that evening, we got a call from Madeline, which I happened to field. Here's pretty much how the conversation went down:

"Hi, Pam. This is Madeline."

"Hi, Madeline."

"Listen, Pam, you seem like a reasonable person."

"I like to think so." (I was beginning to doubt it.)

"Just tell me this." A pregnant pause. "Is she for real?"

Good question!

I thought about it. I weighed my words. The last thing Kim or I wanted, after all we'd been through and put others through, was to mislead someone into investing $500,000 that they might never see again. And, the truth was, any faith we still had in Candi going into that meeting was pretty much obliterated by her behavior. Yes, we had an obligation to development investors, to crew, to cast, to ourselves, to give Candi more time to come up with her promised millions. But we were no longer feeling right about asking anyone for bridge money based on Candi's unmanifested promises. As far as we were concerned, Candi would have to come up with all the money… or none of it at all.

So, was she for real?

"I honestly don't know," I answered. "I wish I could tell you differently."

There was more to the conversation, but that was the most relevant part, and the part that ended it – amicably, but irrevocably.

———

On Nov. 22nd, our payroll company terminated payroll. At this point, we owed a total of about $151,000 to payroll alone.

In the absence of (but anticipation of) money, the Art Department was shut down and a new start date for production announced – Nov. 29th. In the meantime, the actors all went home for the Thanksgiving Holidays and to await further news. Others took a needed break – if not from their worries, at least from us.

As they did every year, my parents were out of town, enjoying the holiday with my mother's siblings. At our house, the kids helped make the semblance of a Thanksgiving dinner, and for the first time in many years, guests were not invited. Apart from that, I don't remember much of anything about my favorite holiday, except that it lacked the carefree spirit of years past, when I would spend days cooking up a storm for family, friends and anyone else who didn't have family nearby with whom to celebrate.

Thanksgiving was typically a big holiday for Kim too and, as usual, her sister had whipped up a wonderful turkey dinner with all the fixings. But to Kim, everything seemed shrouded in invisible heaviness, and she felt completely removed from the festivities.

But we were relatively strong and healthy. We had the love of family, and faith in the long-term future, even as the short-term future threatened to go up in flames. In short, there was still plenty for which to be grateful.

Back from Thanksgiving break on Nov. 27th, Kim and I were quickly faced with a daunting memo, detailing funding requirements in the amount of $536,438.50. A memo from one of the department heads suggested everyone personally contact the Executive Producer (Candi), Producers (Kim and me) and Co-Producer (Gloria) to receive their due payment. I can't imagine that anyone (especially the author of the memo) really believed we could personally provide people their "due payment", but the memo was a way of making sure people knew—if they didn't know it already – where to take their grievances. Up until recently, Ron was their go-to-guy, the guy running the show, at least overtly. Now, as bleak reality was starting to show its face in earnest, the focus was on the legally responsible parties (ourselves), and Ron quite naturally started to take his place on the sidelines, away from the whole nasty mess. But let's face it – at the end of the day, it was our mess to sort out, not his.

In the meantime, certain members of the construction and set decorating department, as well as a few other crew members, contacted the Colorado Department of Labor, requesting wage claim forms. The end result of all the upheaval was a temporary shutdown with a revised start date of Dec. 4th – realistic according to Candi's continued assurances.

(As all of this was going down, some hopeful soul was still working on music clearances. *The beat goes on!*)

By the time the Dec. 4th deadline came and went, Candi had run through a litany of questionable characters in her quest to come up with the needed cash. (*Enter the Viper* and a host of others.) Finally, she brought a player to the table who seemed a grade above the others. Nico arrived amid the growing chaos to sort out Candi's breach of contract and procure the money for her (and, by extension, us) – but not before a key crew member mustered up a certain amount of justifiable indignation and hit us with, "You'll never get work in this town again!" Maybe not, though *never* is certainly a long time. But that was the least of our worries.

On Dec. 18th, Ron sent Nico "everything", that is to say all facts and figures relevant to the film which might be useful in procuring funding. At that point, it was estimated that the current budget would be "closer to $4 million or above, depending on the start date penalties and other encumbrances that the slow-down has engendered." Apart from Candi, no one had met Nico in person. In fact, he operated from another state. But, distance aside, he came on board with the polished attitude and über-confidence of a savior. Just what everyone needed!

As final studio shutdown approached on Dec. 20th, Kim and I were starting to be threatened with lawsuits. Things were looking gloomy, indeed. *Not to worry,* Nico encouraged us, as he reassured us that we were going to do this thing. That being the case, shutdown would not be viewed as the end, but as a way of stopping the accumulation of debt while things could be restructured and revived.

And, yes, the set would be torn down. But – no reason to fear! The phoenix would rise again.

---

1 – Were any photographs ever taken? There must have been, even if the process was cut short. Still, whatever there might have been is nowhere to be found by Kim and me.

LAST-DITCH EFFORTS
Marty's Leg to Stand On

Late November – *It's been a long, arduous, torturous month. But we haven't given up. Hope springs eternal, at least in our own hearts, if not in the hearts of our associates. Battered and buffeted as we feel, the potential end of the project is hard to conceive of and even more difficult to accept. Is it really possible that our beloved song and dance man might never get a chance to sing and dance his way into the hearts of a movie audience? Is it really possible that A Bucket of Paint might never see the light of day?*

True to form, Nigel took it upon himself to try to save the day by making a video – a personal tour of the not-yet-finished but still-standing Victorian house, guided and narrated by Nigel himself, giving the viewer an idea of what the film was about, its tone, what made it special. The idea was to use the video to make some financial appeals. To rescue the project while there was still time. Wouldn't *someone* come forward and be our angel?

Now, at the final hour, Kim and I (and, for a while, Gloria) continued to make calls, send letters, do whatever we possibly could do to save our dying production. Looking back, the ends to which we went would almost be laughable – embarrassing, really – if there weren't also something to be admired in that kind of never-say-die spirit. (Not that anyone was inclined to admire us.) We holed up in our fortress, away from the disparaging crowd (it really wasn't a crowd anymore), putting our heads together, coming up with wild ideas and – what was there to lose? – pursuing them to the bitter end.

Here are excerpts of a letter we sent to just about anyone who might be in a position to help us:

On behalf of all the investors who saw us through the development of the A BUCKET OF PAINT feature film project and who have asked us in all their naiveté and hopefulness, "BUT HAVE YOU TALKED TO OPRAH, JODIE FOSTER, STEVEN SPIELBERG, ETC.?", we are reaching for the stars and appealing to you now... one week before the potential demise of our project.

With all of the violence so prevalent in today's society, we had looked forward with great anticipation to the making of this funny, warm-hearted family film that includes some of the best Irish music by some of the most talented musicians in the world...

There is no way to put into words the time, effort, and financial and emotional expense that have gone into bringing this worthwhile project from its inception to the doorstep of reality – three years of effort from two women who are anything but dilettantes must equal the inexpressible...

Despite their patience, some creditors have had no choice but to take action and there are several lawsuits under way. We are confident that all legal actions will be dropped and creditors satisfied on payment of money owed...

As a last and obviously desperate attempt to save our project, we are writing you, looking for an angel, an investor coming in from the heart and without great delay...

Okay. Now we really are embarrassed.

Needless to say, desperation (not to mention the word *lawsuit*) is a turn-off to all but the most empathetic ear.

———

It was around this time that Kim's sister, who worked in the vicinity, decided to pay us a visit, bringing with her a work associate, a tall, nice-looking man in his thirties, who, like her, was curious about our production. Neither one of them had any idea that things had taken a seriously bad turn, and the cheerful obliviousness they brought to the premises that day was almost unsettling. Kim managed to find a moment to greet them, then pointed them toward the set. Later, Kim would confess that she couldn't even recall the gentleman's name, or his face for that matter – she was that distracted. Waving a hasty goodbye, she did a U-turn and rushed back to the fortress and the herculean task at hand.

On our invitation, the Film Commissioner for the state of Colorado met with us. We weren't entirely hopeful that he could find a way to save what might have been a meaningful contribution to Colorado film at the time, but whatever hopes we did have were pretty quickly dashed. While he expressed his sympathy, he didn't feel there was anything he could do for us. Well, at least we had kept him in the loop.

So, what were our advisors telling us at this time? And would all the advisors in the world have made a difference? Would the captain of the Titanic have benefited from some well-placed advice after the ship hit the iceberg, or would it have been just so much hot air on an irreversibly frigid night? Kim and I had surrounded ourselves early on with what we thought we would need to make sure we were making wise decisions. Almost from the beginning, our advisory pool was made up of a well-rounded and respectable triumvirate that included:

Ron, our Line Producer
Marty, our Attorney
Bob, our Business Advisor

Sounds like a good safety net. And yet it wasn't.
So, what went wrong?
Well, the first thing that went wrong has been touched on before, probably a few times (but not as many times as we've replayed it in

our minds). Though we had development money in place to pay our current and some future expenses, we gave in to Ron and allowed him to move ahead in ways that, due to later complications, would ultimately exceed our bank account. We could have survived even that critical misstep had agreements not been made with the actors that took first monies away from our investor, and had we not gone along with this without a proper fight. Lastly, we should never have agreed to take what seemed like the only expedient way and gone with Candi over our original investor.

The thing about bad decisions is that they breed not only desperation, but their ugly offshoots – more bad decisions. Still, Kim and I could have changed the entire trajectory of our production at the onset. Even if we were tempted to blindly follow the advice of someone more versed in the industry than we were – even if we were torn about which way to go – even if we felt pressured and teetered at the brink of a horrible decision – we should never have moved ahead without first seeking the advice of counsel, by which I mean the overruling counsel of our film-wise entertainment attorney – at *every* important juncture. We should have made the call to Marty and gotten back to Ron with Marty's leg to stand on. Ron might not have been happy with our decisions, but it is most likely that he would have acquiesced and, at the end of the day, enjoyed a successful production alongside us.

Although we had taken the steps to secure three people whose wisdom and experience were important to us, we never took the time to figure out exactly how that was going to work. We didn't have a valid system in place – a system which, at its most effective, might have looked something like this:

RON SUGGESTS PLAN A - Talk to Marty first, let Ron know our decision, then move forward accordingly.

OR, *in another scenario...*

> *WE OURSELVES COME UP WITH PLAN A - Talk to Bob, then talk to Marty, then decide on a course of action, then inform Ron of decision, then move forward accordingly.*

Instead, the system (or lack of it) that we defaulted to went something like this:

> *RON SUGGESTS PLAN A* - Defer to Plan A against our better judgment, then inform Marty of decision made. Lastly, inform Bob of events over a cup of coffee and a glazed almond biscotti.

OR...

> *WE OURSELVES COME UP WITH PLAN A* - Let Ron talk us out of it – then, when there's nothing they can do about it, apprise Marty and Bob of the situation.

The above assessment may be an over-simplified and self-deprecating version of the way we were operating, but there's still a glaring truth in there that boils down to simply this: despite our hard work and early success, we didn't trust ourselves all the way to the finish line, and we didn't harness and effectively utilize our advisory pool (specifically, Marty and Bob) when it might have made the difference. Lesson learned the prehistoric way.

Of course, there was also the nefarious fog that rolled in and enveloped us, sucking our brains out in the process. There's that explanation too.

―――

And then there was Kelly – let us not forget Kelly! – the guy who found us our production investor and who acted as our intermediary during the investment process. A nicer guy there never was. Now, maybe he didn't have money invested in our project, but given his contracted 10% finder's fee, he certainly stood to make a substantial amount if things went right. Yet, no matter how grim things looked, Kelly never had a mean word to say to us, nor a cold shoulder to plant between himself and the two people who heaved a bucket of paint over his fondest expectations.

———

One day, while we were still frantically working on leads, still trying hard to resurrect the film, but also on the cusp of accepting hard reality, Bob came by to see us. He had just returned from a trip down south where he had taken the opportunity to meet with our initial investor (the real one, not the candi-coated one). Bob sat down, got comfortable, and looked us meaningfully in the eye. "She was for real," he said. (Past tense, of course. She was out of the picture by now.) But this was no revelation to us. We had never doubted that she was for real. She was about as real as they come in an industry where even would-be investors are too often part of the overall illusion. And, unlike so many investors who care more about having a big name attached to a film than in the quality of the film itself, she had always reiterated her stance and firmly stood her ground -- what mattered most to her were the budget and the script. Get that right. Then, based on that solid foundation, go for the best possible actors you can get.

Sadly, she was no longer an option.

THE LONGEST DAY
The Day of the Frozen Parakeets

Dec. 20th 1995 – *All good things must come to an end. Bad ones too, thank goodness. Which brings to mind my mother's favorite words from the Bible – "And it came to pass..." – words she found comforting because they reminded her that not even the deepest sorrow goes on forever. As a Buddhist, the words of comfort that I find myself clinging to at this time are from the 13th Century monk, Nichiren, who said, "Suffer what there is to suffer, enjoy what there is to enjoy. Regard both suffering and joy as facts of life, and continue chanting Nam-myoho-renge-kyo, no matter what happens."*

In essence – keep the faith, and even in the midst of your suffering, don't forget to appreciate the joy that comes your way.

Not always an easy task, but definitely worth the effort.

The last day at the studio was upon us.

Kim and I weren't done trying to rescue our project – in fact, a mountain of hardships and challenges still lay ahead – but the production itself had to come to a grinding halt. The owner of the studio, though courteous and civilized given the circumstances, clearly wanted us to vacate the premises ASAP to make way for paying clientele. No one wanted to stay at this point, anyway. Yes, there were still a few who held on to the faint hope that Kim and I would find a way to resurrect the project, but that wasn't their job – it was ours. Most of the crew just wanted to go have a beer (with a chaser) and forget they'd ever linked their fates to ours.

By this time, I don't think it's an exaggeration to say that Kim and I were viewed as pariahs.

Still, I would be remiss if I didn't mention that there had been one attempt, sometime before, at enveloping us in the fold. It happened during one of our "morning meetings". Being of a slightly over-sensitive nature, I had always worked very hard not to break down during these trying sessions. And, up until then, I had been successful in my quest, the herculean task at hand (raising the phoenix) taking precedence over the self-indulgent act of falling apart.

But the clock was ticking and my holding-it-together time was just about up. As my head swam around in the painful reality (and unreality) of it all, Nigel suddenly exclaimed in an unexpectedly booming voice, "You never say *ANYTHING!*"

Me?

Putting the slight exaggeration aside, he was right, of course. But there was a reason I held my tongue – which was this: short of being able to produce the money, there was very little I could say that would satisfy anyone. And, not being (for lack of better words) a bullshitter, there was very little that I *wanted* to say. In short, much as everyone needed placating, I had no placating words to offer. And nor did Kim. Thus, we did what we always did – listened, took the blows, weathered the bad vibes, waited for the meeting to end, and went back to trying to make something happen.

But I was shaken by Nigel's voice. Not sure why, but I've always gotten a chill down my spine when a grown man (is that redundant?) yells at me, and once even pissed my pants – well, not the whole bladder-full, but just enough to feel privately embarrassed about it – when my boss walked by my desk, taking me by surprise and yelling about something or other having nothing to do with me. True, Nigel wasn't yelling in any earth-shattering sense – but this *did* have something to do with me, and I was definitely shaken.

I looked over at Kim. I could see understanding in her eyes, but also the hard line. The reminder that I needed to keep it together.

At this point, I knew that if I opened my mouth, it would all be over. Endless days of emotional wear and tear were having their impact, and a flood of tears was waiting at the levee. The eyes of everyone in the room were upon me. *Yeah – why doesn't she ever say anything?*

Was I going to say something now?

I opened my mouth to say – who knows what? – when Kim pre-empted me. To this day, neither one of us remembers exactly what she said – or what I said, because I did eventually utter something. Suffice it to say it was enough to break the levee and unleash the flood of tears. To her credit, Kim held it together. I, on the other hand, was unstoppable.

When I was a kid, my oldest brother used to accuse me of saving up my tears for when my father got home, i.e., being able to turn on the water works at will. I guess there's some truth to that, though it's not as calculated as it sounds. Growing up with three brothers and a mother who favored the boys, I learned to hold on to my emotions until such a time as I knew I had a sympathetic ear, i.e., my oft-traveling father's.

Miss you, Pop!

Don't get me wrong. During the demise of *A Bucket of Paint*, I cried a lot. But I did as I always had. I chose my moment. And that moment was always on safe turf. At home. In front of my dogs. In front of my family. In front of my altar. Alone under the stars. In the bathtub.

But on that particular day I was no longer able to hold it in. Tears didn't roll gently down my cheeks, but literally exploded from my eyes, soaking everyone in the vicinity with my unabashed anguish. My eyes swelled up. My nose swelled up. I flashed on my mother's having once told me – in a botched attempt at encouraging me to just smile and be happy – that I wasn't pretty when I cried. Which, of course, just made me feel ugly and gave me more reason to cry.

After a few moments of this – or an eternity, depending on whom you ask – Nigel made his way to my chair, kneeled at my feet, and enveloped me in his arms in a vain attempt to soothe the savage beast. It was very dear of him, his cheek was warm and comforting against mine, but I felt on display, and anyway, no words of sympathy could quell me. At this point, I just had to cry it out.

At the end of which there was still no money.

I'm sure my behavior was a little shocking to everyone present, Kim included. But, eventually, the long, unprofessional moment was over, and someone said – maybe it was Nigel, but neither Kim, nor I, can remember – *why don't we all go out and get a bite to eat?* It was an odd feeling to be included in the invitation (we never had been) and, telepathically, Kim and I concurred that it would be the right thing to do under the circumstances. I pulled myself together and we all went out the door.

It was one of the most miserable lunches Kim and I have ever endured. Nice gesture. Poor execution. But I guess we were all trying in the best way we knew how.

———

So, here we were on the last day at the studio. People had packed up and left, or were packing up and leaving. Unlike the way things played themselves out in our fantasies, it wasn't a day of celebration, or even a day of fond farewells, but rather a day of icy goodbyes, or goodbyes coldly left unsaid. People had been hurt. *By us.* For some, we had crushed a dream. Granted, it was our dream, but we had shared it with them and brought them into it, and failed to take it to the finish line. Those were the facts, and though there still lingered a modicum of hope, it was a bitter pill to swallow.

Mabrey, our Production Coordinator, who had remained professional until the end, helped load boxes into our cars. Her friendliness toward us (she was, by nature, sweet and friendly) had waned in the last couple of weeks, but we could still count on her to see things through. It was sad to feel her pull away. Even so, we never felt anything but gratitude for her steady presence.

Mabrey's professionalism aside, that last day at the studio was a cold and dreary day in hell. Yet, even in the midst of our personal suffering, joy and laughter were still to be found!

As we wandered aimlessly through the hallways for the last time, taking in, I suppose, the inevitability of it all, two people approached us, their demeanor surprisingly sweet and solicitous. They obviously hadn't gotten the memo.

"Pam and Kim – hi!"

Mark and Suzette had only one ambition – one last mission, if you will. To find out what the producers wanted done with their frozen parakeets.

Mark and Suzette were understandably proud of their parakeets (which were to factor into the film), had never got to show them off to us personally, and undoubtedly felt a little thwarted that nothing was going to come of them. We took the time to admire the photographs, thanked them for their work, expressed our regret that things hadn't worked out, and then gave the edict that they could dispose of the frozen parakeets at will – or do whatever it is prop masters do with their stock of unused frozen parakeets. For the time being, at least, frozen parakeets were not at the top of our priority list.

It was sweet and innocent and, frankly, surreal. It was also heartening to know that two people still thought well enough of us to take the time to consult with us on our way out the door and to offer their condolences.

Condolences!

It was the fondest of farewells, and I was poignantly reminded to "enjoy what there is to enjoy". We even managed to get a laugh out of it.

―――

Mabrey had left, and now it was time for Kim and I to part. Well, just for the evening, but still. We might never be going back to the studio – to the set – to the once-joy – even to the now-pain. Our work was nowhere near done, but it would be different from now on. It would be harder.

I tucked in the last box and closed the trunk of my car. Kim closed hers. Then, looking up at me with tears in her eyes, she said with a fervor I'll never forget, "Pam you're the *best* partner anyone could ever have!" The feeling was, of course, quite mutual, which I expressed with tears in my own eyes. We'd been through rough times, we'd let our beloved project slip through our fingers, and most of the people we'd worked with now completely dismissed us as ne'er-do-wells, or worse yet, deeply and bitterly disliked us.

But we knew who we were, and come what may, we still had faith in each other.

INTERMISSION

Time for some popcorn!

ACT TWO

RUN, DOG, RUN – The Money's Coming on Monday

NO MORE MR. NICE GUY – Things Get Really Ugly

THE HELIX HOTEL FIASCO – A New Low

LAWSUITS AND BROKEN BONES – Flying High and Landing Hard

WHEN THE GOING GETS TOUGH – Personal Bankruptcy

STAYING ALIVE – From La-La Land to a Federation of the World

MAY IT PLEASE THE COURT – Corporate Bankruptcy

AFTERSHOCK – Dealing with Internal Injuries

CATCHING FIREFLIES – The Oxygen Bra and Other Inspirations

LIFE GOES ON – Kim Finally Gets a Pedicure

RUN, DOG, RUN
The Money's Coming on Monday

January 1996 — *Well, we may have left the studio, but we still haven't given up. That's because Candi's latest moneyed connection, the aforementioned Nico, is still at it — zealously, it seems. In critical breach of contract, Candi claims endlessly that she, and he, are going to get it done — that the money is — hang on to your hats — forthcoming. We've come to view Candi as a loose cannon, but we're still not sure what Nico is, though we wonder if he's just a master of distraction. His voice is confident and strangely calming — mesmerizing even. The fact that he is apparently closely linked to Candi is, ironically, something of a red flag, but he sounds like a decent guy (at least over the phone) and, if he isn't the real thing, gives a good imitation of legitimacy. Kim does her best to verify everything he tells us — which is a lot to follow, and to swallow — but it's not an easy job, given that we have limited means to keep paying for background checks or legal counsel.*

Thanksgiving had been bleak, but Christmas would be even bleaker, not just for ourselves, but for everyone concerned. Believe me, it's not a happy feeling to know that you've thrown a stink bomb into everyone's Christmas.

Kim's Christmas that year remains a blur. "My Mom and older sister were very supportive and helped me out," she vaguely remembers. "I cried a lot."

Aware that there would be no presents at our house this year, Gloria very sweetly wrapped up a number of items lying around her house so that our kids would have presents under the tree. It was thoughtful of her, and gave a little fun for the kids. But all Kim and I really wanted was for Christmas to end so that we could get back to the task at hand – the task that never took time off from our psyche – somehow getting money into the bank so we could pay arrears, so things could start up again, so the project and everyone attached to it could be saved. It was a long shot, we knew that, but Nico assured us it could be done – *would be done!* – and in short order.

So, who was this Nico, at the end of the day?

Well, for one thing, Nico was the originator (maybe not the originator, but he said them a lot) of such memorable maxims as:

- *The flesh is weak*
- *Never apologize in Hollywood*

AND

- *The money's coming on Monday*

Nico was the man who kept us waiting by the fax machine for items critical to the funding of *A Bucket of Paint* – items he alternately referred to as:

- the Paperwork
- the Codes
- the Commitment Letter
- the Specimen
- the Guarantee
- the IPP
- the Subscription Agreement

AND, of course,

- the Binder

In my spinning head, poetry was beginning to foment. Ditties like:

- Things will be better when we get that letter.
- We'll be out of the grinder when we get that binder.

And of course,

We'll have to explode if we don't get that code.

To be fair, the process of exploding (or rather, imploding) had already begun well before Nico made his advent into our midst. He was just the guy we chose to believe in when Candi dropped the ball – *did Candi ever have the ball?* – the guy who kept us believing we could somehow put the pieces of the implosion back together. *Is it possible to put an implosion back together?*

We do know this much about Nico. He lived in Massachusetts, or Delaware, or possibly both (but not simultaneously), and he was somehow more than superficially connected to Candi. Was it by blood? Was Nico somehow indebted to her? Lacking sustenance, our imaginations had no choice but to run wild.

We did inquire about his connection to Candi, but got one of those long-winded answers that leaves you wondering if there's something wrong with your own brain for not understanding a word that's being said. Nico hinted at Candi's having held a high-level position in a mutual business enterprise, but we had to assume this harked back to a previous existence, since at this point, truth be told, Candi was barely able to hold her own in a business conversation.

When Candi first brought Nico into the equation, she acted as our interface, but, by necessity, we eventually took to speaking with him directly. As previously mentioned, Nico was a calm, reassuring voice in the wilderness. He didn't seem to pack any extra water bottles for his friends, but the images he painted were of palm trees swaying in the wind over large pools of clear, sparkling water where everyone's thirst would sooner or later be quenched.

We weren't the only ones still talking to Nico. Ron and Nigel occasionally touched base with him too. In January, when Nico was supposed to be arranging an advance, Nigel met with him in person and subsequently drew a tentative, but encouraging, portrait of the man. Nico seemed very honest; schooled his children at home; his father was a postman, his mother a social worker; he was concerned about women's rights... How perfect was this guy? Maybe the money really would come in on Monday.)

Eager to get the money flowing, even the payroll company we employed eventually started making its own calls to Nico who was, at least early on – despite the fact that he had us all gnawing at our fingernails – an apparently popular guy. For a while, everyone seemed to think he might actually come through. Maybe not on Monday, but truly, any day of the week would have been acceptable. At the least, Nico seemed to be well-connected in the industry.

Listening to reports of seriously interested investors – waiting for codes and binders coming in – standing by the fax machine in expectation – scrambling to provide Nico with yet another budget tweak or some other urgently required piece of documentation – gut-wrenching disappointment that was always mitigated by reports of yet another interested party – began in the days before our departure from the studio and continued well after we had vacated the premises.

Was it a game? And, if it was a game, what did Nico stand to gain? Why would he put so much effort into the charade, if indeed it was one? What did Candi stand to gain – or maybe not to lose?

Frustrating and infuriating as it was, we wanted desperately to believe it was for real.

NO MORE MR. NICE GUY
Things Get Really Ugly

January 1996: *The question of where to go from here (at least, physically) has been answered — well, sort of. Paige (the woman who had inspired us with her talk of circling the wagons and making baked beans) has offered me a part-time receptionist position with her acting school, with the understanding that Kim will come over as much as possible to continue the work of interfacing with Nico and responding to his requests, and that I will join her in my down time and/or off hours. It's a kind offer on Paige's part, and one which serves my needs (to some degree) as — lacking the support we've always depended on from my income, and in up to our ears — my family's financial situation is getting dire. Kim, on the other hand, won't have a job at the school, per se, and I feel badly about that. Not insignificantly, this arrangement will allow Paige to keep tabs on our progress. Given the fact that she has a substantial amount of money invested, we completely understand how important this is to her, and still cling to the sliver of hope that we can turn things around.*

By early January, the owner of the studio informed us that 70% of the set had been torn down and that we needed plastic wrap to cover the big pieces piled high outside the studio. He also provided us with a tally of our outstanding bills, a figure that towered just about as high as the fractured set. We made an appointment to speak with him personally, not to plead our case, but to let him know firsthand where things stood and to turn in our keys (yes, we'd finally gotten keys!). Naturally, he wasn't pleased with what we had to say, but under the circumstances, he was kind enough, and we appreciated his show of decency.

Meantime, Nico was busy at work – or seemed to be. Early January was replete with his promises and optimism, and on January 20th, he sent us a letter, which we immediately forwarded to the payroll company, detailing a "money commitment" of $500,000. A few days later, Nico informed us that his "group" in California had verbally agreed to finance the balance of the picture. Kim and I quickly passed on this information to the attorney representing one of the suing crew members. The attorney said he would advise his client and promised not to take any action until the following week.

On the same day, one of the major support services we were using informed us that they were going to "go to the District Attorney" unless we supplied them with a personal guarantee. It was clear, however, that the only things of value Kim and I had with which to underwrite a personal guarantee were our respective homes, though there wasn't that much equity in either of them. This particular company was only doing what it needed to do to secure its interests. Still, the threat didn't sit easy on our ears.

I'd already made the mistake of signing a personal guarantee for lumber. This time, however, neither one of us was about to sign on the dotted line. We were a corporation, after all. Let the lawsuits fall where they may, there would be no more personal guarantees from either of us.

Despite Nico's unflagging optimism, things were getting pretty unpleasant. Kim received a call from the Set Dressing Department and gave the individual in question (Hank) the update from Nico. Hank replied that his vendors couldn't hold off anymore and that he had gone ahead and paid them by personal check, which he had mailed on Friday with the three-day weekend in his favor. He cautioned that the money had better be in his hands by 5:00 p.m. or else "all hell would break loose" and finished by saying, "That's all I have to say." To which he added that he wasn't going to be "Mr. Nice Guy" anymore. At which point he hung up. Kim was stunned. Why hadn't he talked to us first? Why hadn't he let us deal with the vendors? The debt was ours, not his. We had certainly not approved such an action and were helpless to do anything about it, much the less pay him back by 5:00 p.m.

The mood took a turn for the worse when Kim discovered that production items were being stolen, along with an extensive CD collection belonging to our Assistant Director. We were shocked. What was stealing going to accomplish? Were people helping themselves to whatever they could get their hands on as some sort of (in their minds) defensible payback? If so, it made no sense to steal from the Assistant Director, who was, for all intents and purposes, one of them. Why target a guy who just did his job, never had a harsh word for anyone, and wasn't responsible for the situation? When we asked Ron about the whole affair, his only response was, "What do you expect?"

And then, in late February, Ron began to join the personal outcry for money.

On March 5, in preparation of a list of owed monies requested by Nico (who was always requesting some list or other), Ron prepared his own "invoice". Kim specifically asked him not to send this to Nico, but rather to allow us to incorporate it into our own list, which we would then send to Nico.

Ron sent his own list anyway and thusly expressed his feelings about the actors getting paid: "They aren't hurting. They can wait." As such, they were left off his list. Specifically, Ron's list called for Nigel to receive $23,000, Ron $5,000 and Pam & Kim $2,500 each. We'd never been on the payroll, so this was an interesting twist. These were not figures he had discussed with us. According to our notes of the time, Kim expressed her feeling and mine that, if anyone was going to get paid, the construction workers should get paid, to which Ron replied that they could wait, that he was a worker too.

Meantime, Nigel used his own resources and looked for funding from contacts he knew in London and elsewhere. But the hardship, both financial and emotional, was taking its toll. His frustration was understandable. We weren't happy about the situation either, especially since, apart from feeling bad about it, we couldn't do any more for him than we could for anyone else.

Although Ron had received full paychecks all along, he was now crying out for money that wasn't forthcoming.

He wasn't the only one.

On March 8th we received a phone call from a crew member who informed us that he wanted full payment or he would "go ballistic". We weren't exactly sure what ballistic meant in this context, but it certainly had a threatening ring. Here's urbandictionary.com's definition of the word:

"to be extremely and uncontrollably furious

(as in)

Fred went ballistic, and managed to punch 5 holes in the wall, in addition to throwing a microwave halfway across his house."

Quite frankly, the situation was beginning to feel a little scary.

Around that time, we received yet another phone message from Hank:

"I have a bill here for $49. I need this taken care of immediately…it's one thing that you just don't pay people and that you screw up people's lives by just leaving them hanging like you've done. But if this bill comes to any sort of collection or anything, you know I will find you people. I will sue you people if it's the last damn thing I do on earth."

Given the fact that Hank had spent his own money to pay down vendors, the $49 mentioned here was just the tip of the iceberg – or more accurately, the volcano.

The atmosphere was becoming palpably explosive.

Urgency nipping at our heels, we asked Nico (not for the first time) if we could speak with his contacts directly or obtain some written proof to substantiate his promises. His reply was that he only "wished" he could divulge all the information, but could not. In the spirit of the best defense being a good offense, he added, "You don't realize how much we are doing for you." If the "we" of which he spoke, included Candi, Kim and I could only shake our heads and say, in the parlance of the day.... *whatever.* (Eventually, Kim and I would tell Nico and Candi that, in order for us to continue working with Nico in good faith, Candi would have to step out of the picture – at least as far as we were concerned. Frankly, at that point, we just couldn't stomach seeing or hearing from her anymore.)

Candi's eventual departure from our daily lives notwithstanding, the nine months we spent replying to Nico's myriad requests for documentation and listening to his animated promises were nothing short of a nauseating roller coaster ride. Per the log Kim kept of our phone calls at the time, here's just a sampling of the ride we took, courtesy of Nico.

Jan 5 – Things are improving by the minute.

Jan 5 – Will be on the phone this afternoon… impressed and do-able.

Jan 16 - Paperwork is being done… may be (until) tomorrow that we receive a fax.

Jan 22 – Reviewed *A Bucket of Paint* package and was impressed... meeting is set for this afternoon... contract with Paramount for a 3 picture $15M deal... thinks *A Bucket of Paint* will fit in.

Feb 6 – May get the money today - real interest from Hollywood guy.

Feb 6 – The funds should come in tomorrow in the Merrill Lynch account.

Feb 7 – LOOKS LIKE MONEY TOMORROW - IN MERRILL LYNCH ACCOUNT

Feb 28 - Making headway - money is coming in...

Feb 28 - API will produce it... If API doesn't work out - Prelude.

Feb 29 – Working on Prelude... VG money seems to be coming together... paperwork and money in place tomorrow.

Feb 29 – Specimen won't be ready until tomorrow.

Feb 29 – The specimen is in place... expect the money by MONDAY.

March 5 – Going to have a conversation with RG in 1/2 hour re release of funds.

March 5 – Sent package to MK at Prelude... going well.

March 5 – Tomorrow either Check or Notification... Verbal commitment from Prelude.

March 8 – Financial structure coming in - process will include payment.

March 8 – Working with Prelude ... will have access to P&A and Distribution.

March 13 – No communications until MONDAY... 2-3 clauses being worked on until MONDAY.

March 28 – VG may give go ahead as early as today... may go to Palm Beach tomorrow to meet with C and pick up Binder... trying to get distribution in -place.

April 1 – Processing the binder... Picking up residency of MGM/UA. We are getting paid this week.

April 3 – Receiving the final funds.

April 3 – Received Binder from C. Will review for compliance.

April 4 – No transfer of money tomorrow (Friday) because it's Good Friday and the banks are closed.

April 4 – MONDAY or Tuesday or Wednesday... should have the money.

April 12 – Execution of letter on Tuesday... They will release funds... Subscription is available.

April 17 – Ready to pick up letter.

April 22 – Transfer of funds early as tomorrow.

April 22 – Nico says this week.

April 23 – Papers were sent to VG yesterday.

Undated – 3.7M Monies promised.

April 25 – May 1st closing date. They will send paperwork.... Nico will fax P&K the Subscription Offer.

April 25 - VG is proceeding with the subscription agreement.

May 1 - As we speak, they are working on the paperwork.

May 2 – Still waiting for Don... everything is moving forward.

May 3 – We will be advised about money on MONDAY... Copy of subscription on MONDAY.

May 3 – Will call on MONDAY to confirm the funds are available.

May 3 – Have funds the MONDAY after Mother's Day... subscription today or tomorrow.

May 7 – Agreements will be out this week. MONDAY May 13th funds are available.

May 10 – Funding ...definitely be available on MONDAY.

July 2 – Letter of Intent finance 100%... Wants to be Partner as opposed to owner.

July 8 – Might have been approved 1 1/2 hours ago... Will provide a draft of the paperwork...

July 15 – Heading bank tomorrow. Money moving tomorrow.

July 16 – It's going well.

July 19 – Chairman of the Board is meeting w/ Nico.

Aug 24 – Monies have been committed.

Sep 2 – Fax is forthcoming.

How's your stomach? Mine's still churning.

It didn't help that Nico began just about every conversation by addressing us as, "Ladies!" Of course, women are referred to as "ladies" all the time in contexts that are not the least bit offensive to either Kim or me. The coffee shop, the grocery store, the hair salon. And then there's the "ladies' room", which we gratefully acknowledge as our own. But with Nico, the word had a different feel to it. It irritated our sensibilities. Not the first time he said it, of course. The first time was fine. Not the second time either. Or even the third or fourth time. The fifth time was fine too. It was the 256th time that put our knickers in a wad.

Any reasonable person reading the above litany of promises would have to wonder how we could have continued to listen to Nico's rhetoric, much the less still believed anything he had to say. Sifting through the phone conversations twenty years later, we ourselves wonder the same thing (with more than a hint of discomfiture). It must be noted, however, that we were, at the time, utterly and completely wrapped up in the tempest of a multi-million-dollar project that was desperately in need of rescue and, increasingly, caught up in the whirlwind of defending our lives.

It's also important to note that Nico's words, though presented here verbatim, were surrounded by all kinds of explanations and reassurances not presented here (and which would make any reader's head spin), all of which added up to, if not a convincing argument, at least the makings of a morsel of hope (which, when you're starving for good news, will easily serve to tide you over).

There was also the chance that the promises were for real and, though increasingly agonizing to endure and difficult to interpret, still worth listening to. Yet, as the days, weeks and months of torment went by, any faith we might have once had in Nico began to fade, only to be replaced by the wish to be done with him.

SURGERY BY INVESTOR
An Unexpected Visit

January 1996 *– I'm not sure I'm the greatest assistant Paige has ever had, but I do my best. Days roll by in a painful sameness. Nico is still "working" at it, but it's just more of same — only with different players attached. We'd be bored and annoyed, if not downright pissed off, if it weren't for the fact that we're still riding the hope train and not yet ready to jump off. I'm sure Paige is getting just as tired of the situation as we are, as our faces can only serve as an uncomfortable reminder of the financial injury she has suffered and for which succor does not seem imminent.*

The best news of the day comes when I win $40 on my $2 scratch ticket. Kim and I are excited. It's the closest either one of us has come in months to a relationship with actual money. For one disjointed moment, I wonder if we shouldn't be distributing the winnings — a pretty silly idea, which I instantly dismiss in favor of buying a Swiss cheese and avocado sandwich with a side of coleslaw.

One evening, as Kim and I labored over some new busywork Nico had conjured up for us (making sure we remained busy was *de rigueur*, as it kept us both hopeful and pre-occupied), Ron and Nigel paid us a visit. They were friendly enough, but then Nigel had always done his best to remain friendly. Ron, though, was a little too friendly. Something was definitely up.

    We braced ourselves (for what, we weren't sure) as they took a seat across from us, looking quite serious and intent, but also oddly sympathetic — the way a doctor might look at you to tell you the bad news. I felt myself squirm in my chair — and yet, my curiosity was greater than my discomfort. Kim too was all ears. What bad news could there be that we hadn't heard already?

We won't try to reconstruct dialogue here, as we would be hard-pressed to remember enough of it to render it authentic. The essence of it, however, remains clear, and Ron took the lead in expressing it. They wanted us to consider relinquishing the project to them.

We were stunned – dazed and confused, actually – and then we simply took a sort of knee-jerk offense to the suggestion. It could be argued that this was a mercy mission, if not on our behalf, then on the project's. Still, we couldn't figure out how a change of hands would make a difference.

At some point in the conversation, Kim spoke up to defend her devotion to the project and, ultimately, her love of film itself, stating (as she wandered a little off topic) that one day she herself wanted to direct a film. No sooner were the words out of her mouth, but that she realized how flip they sounded.

Too late! Nigel's jaw dropped in a show of utter disbelief.

His reaction, while understandable, was painful to Kim at a time when she was not only dealing with the stress of our situation, but also dealing with health issues that had culminated in the need for surgery. As fate would have it, surgery would be at the hands of a skilled doctor who happened to be one of our heftiest development investors (she wasn't hefty, the investment was) – the one who, not that long ago, had sent Jagan to intern at the studio. *Oh, the irony!*

The meeting ended without our having come to any agreement, but truthfully, it was kind of a non-starter to begin with. Perhaps they had thought we would be glad to be relieved of our burden. Undoubtedly, they believed that they really would be doing us, and everyone else, a favor to take it off our hands, though it was never clear exactly how the project could be resurrected, given all its encumbrances.

We could let the project go, having nothing in recompense for all our effort except for an endless barrage of lawsuits, or keep giving it our best shot, despite the unlikeliness of success (and he promise of an endless barrage of lawsuits). Either way, the likeliness of success at this point was pretty remote. Those were the two choices, and we chose the latter.

It goes without saying that Kim's surgeon put aside her losses and operated with even-handed professionalism. Surgery was a success.

The movie, on the other hand, was on its way to code blue.

THE HELIX HOTEL FIASCO
A New Low

August 1996 – *Kim has just received a call from the Helix Hotel, requesting pictures of the actors. Normally, we'd be flattered and happy to comply. Given the current situation, we're downright bewildered. Things have been ugly, but now they're just getting weird.*

Having for many years worked for prominent law firms situated in the heart of Denver, Kim knew the downtown area like the back of her hand. Denver wasn't quite Chicago back then, or the hub that it is now for that matter – but it was, and is, a great city, which even geographically impaired people such as I can navigate with relative ease. With Kim in the lead, we arrived on time for our appointment with the attorneys for the Helix hotel. There was hotel brass present as well – but who exactly everyone was, we'd be hard pressed to remember. I'm not sure I was even aware of it at the time.

Kim and I sat next to each other on one side of the table, sandwiched between dark suits wearing poker-faced expressions. There were pitchers of ice water on the table and individual glasses at each place. This I clearly remember because I was nervous and dry-mouthed and thirsty, but didn't dare move my trembling hand from under the table to pour myself a glass of water for fear I would draw attention to myself, and then (as the nightmare fantasy went) spill the pitcher of ice cold water over the assortment of legal documents that lined the table.

Instead, I tried to exercise my brain. Why had we asked to meet with them? What did we hope to accomplish? Were we gluttons for punishment? What could we say or do to mitigate the situation? Was there a kind heart in the mix? Would anything we said make a difference? And what would be the outcome if we were unable to successfully plead our case?

In short, here was the problem. When the actors (and some crew) had checked into their hotel rooms in November, the Helix had asked to run their personal credit cards. As we all know, this isn't an unusual request when someone checks into a hotel – and most of the actors complied. But since the production company (*Shoe in the Road*) was responsible for the bill, the move was surprising, though Kim and I didn't learn about it until later, when the complications began to surface. At any rate, none of this would have been important had all gone according to plan. Room costs and even minor incidentals would have been paid in full and on time. However, the switch from our original investor to Candi coincided with the general timeframe of check-in, and the money to pay the hotel bill would in the end, given Candi's subsequent default, not be forthcoming.

A horrible situation indeed. But what made it all the more unthinkable was that the Helix, with little qualm or deliberation, had turned around and billed the actors, not just for incidentals, but for their entire stay at the hotel. When Kim and I got wind of this, we were devastated. We understood that the hotel was due its payment, but it was painfully obvious to us that the actors weren't to blame for the default. We were. This shift of responsibility left us feeling at a complete loss.

A personal meeting with the hotel was in order, and we arranged for it to happen. Surely, we could sort this mess out.

Or maybe not.

Kim and I pleaded our case. *The actors aren't at fault. We are.* That was our main chorus, but for better or worse, we also suggested that the hotel might want to take the higher road and just write off the loss. Aren't losses good things to have at tax time? Maybe so, but this isn't exactly what you want to hear from someone who owes you money. Still, the possibility existed and, in our opinion, was worth noting. And wouldn't that be a better scenario than holding the actors personally responsible? This was, after all, a hotel that prided itself on its display of autographed headshots of actors and other luminaries who had stayed there.

But the meeting that Kim and I had hoped for, in which heart-to-heart dialogue would result in some kind of less punitive (for the actors) middle ground, hissed, sputtered and sizzled its way to an embarrassing end. The dark suits were all in agreement with each other – an agreement that had, in all probability, been reached well prior to our meeting, and from which script there was no deviating.

Things would stand as they were. The actors would have to pay.

Kim and I said our goodbyes and left the hotel. We were frustrated. We were upset. But we weren't done. We felt we had an obligation to do everything we could for the actors – not just for the actors, but on behalf of our own self-esteem – though, by now, it was becoming evident that the money was never coming in and that bankruptcy was probably our only way forward. Our final strategy would be to write a letter to the Helix, asking them once again to reconsider charging cast and crew for *Shoe in the Road* expenses. Alone with the letter and a little private time to weigh the options, maybe – just maybe – the person reading it would have a change of heart.

Here are some excerpts of the letter we drafted and sent to the Helix Hotel:

In light of the fact that we stayed in contact with (name withheld) regarding the status of our project and our continued efforts to get it off the ground, we are more than disappointed with your decision to burden our actors and crew members with our debt. Although we were forewarned that after a certain period of time the (Helix) "would have no choice but to take action", it was expected that the action would be taken against Shoe in the Road Productions Inc., and not against our cast and crew members individually.

... we fully acknowledge that our cast and crew may hold us responsible for this unfortunate turn of events, but we wonder if your handling of this situation might also be viewed as unreasonable, if not unethical. It just does not seem fair to us that our cast and crew should suffer the consequences of our financial misfortune.

We hope that you will reconsider this matter with an eye toward fairness and improved public relations by reversing the individual charges. We appreciate your helpfulness...

Our pleas, both in person and in writing, were not successful in moving the Helix to bend its stance. Ironically, soon thereafter, we received a phone message from someone at the Helix, cheerfully requesting we send them autographed headshots of the (*A Bucket of Paint*) actors who had stayed at the hotel. For their walls, you know.

Huh?

Later, when Kim called back asking to speak to a higher-up, the Helix denied the original phone call had ever taken place. Sadly, it had. However, one has to believe that it was a call made in error, perhaps by an administrator who knew only that the actors had stayed there, but wasn't privy to the whole story.

Needless to say, we never sent the pictures.

LAWSUITS AND BROKEN BONES
Flying High and Landing Hard

August 1996 *– Kim has taken on the most unpleasant, but necessary, task of fending off vendors – credit card companies, phone companies, various entities to whom our production company owes money – not to mention a slew of opposing attorneys. She does this weekly, and the result is a lesson in the importance of dialogue. As long as we keep the lines of communication open, updating everyone on our current circumstances, they are by and large patient. People have shown themselves to be (to varying degrees) considerate and understanding. Still, it's not an easy job, and I'm grateful to Kim for being willing to take it on. Over and over and over again.*

Who was it who said, "When you're going through hell, keep on going?"[1]

Granted, hell might have been a lot less agonizing (or, at least, shorter) if we'd simply drawn the line early on and called it quits, but we couldn't bring ourselves to do that until all avenues had been exhausted. This required a certain amount of emotional stamina as well as a willingness to communicate, even with our worst enemies. Maybe we were foolish to persevere; maybe we were something a little more laudable. Maybe it didn't matter what we were. In the end, we simply believed that to keep on going, even to a bitter end, was the key to some deeper victory, whether the victory manifested itself now or decades from now and in some wholly other fashion.

But from March through early September, legal entanglements were the story of the day. The payroll company, the DGA (Directors Guild of America), the car rental company, and various other companies and individuals filed lawsuits against the production company. Thank goodness for Kim and her paralegal background! I have to admit that I have something of a penchant for legal things (legal language included), but there is no doubt that Kim was the bedrock of our court battles. Thanks to her, we were always prepared, paperwork in order, ready to defend our case – which seemed to be appreciated by the courts, regardless of the matter at hand, and regardless of the ruling. And, while the various judges we encountered might not have expressed overt sympathy for us, there seemed to be a quiet respect for our efforts and sincerity. Strangely, the sense of dispassion we experienced in the court system – the detachment, if you will, the neutrality and objectivity – were almost a welcome breath of fresh air.

As the designated registered agent of *Shoe in the Road Productions Inc.,* summonses were delivered to my house.

"Hi there!" would come the friendly greeting at the front door. "Pamela Nelson?"

"Yes?" I would venture, wary, but still friendly in return.

Quickly shifting to the dark side: "You've been served!"

Seldom was the approach more creative than that, though in one case, a summons was thrown at me over the bushes as if it were the morning paper. Guy must have been in a hurry.

Certain members of the construction (and other) crew chose to vent their anger by menacing us; others simply walked away, vowing never to have anything to do with us again. Still, a couple of others went through the court system, seeking restitution for wages lost. Kim and I have often talked about how much we appreciated these last people. They had a fair grievance and they pursued us fairly, without reverting to bodily threats or personal attacks.

Ironically, Kim and I had always felt a special appreciation for the construction workers – maybe because their work was so physical, so behind-the-scenes, and to some degree, so removed from the "glamour" of film. But the truth is, there were members of the construction team, especially at a higher level of responsibility, who never liked us and never sought to hide the fact, even when things were going well for everyone. Whether we passed them in the studio hallway or came to the set for a visit, the vibe from these individuals was openly negative. Kim and I were never sure whether this was a case of blatant misogyny or something even more personal, but we stayed friendly in the hopes that the climate would change. And it did. It got exponentially worse once Candi was in default.

But, as said, not everyone boarded the hate train. In one case, we went through mediation in small claims court with a worker out to recover his due. The court-appointed mediator attempted to find common ground and a workable solution. In the process, she recounted her own heartfelt story – one of hardship and recovery that had left her sympathetic to all sides. She did her best for everyone, even though there wouldn't be much in the way of restitution for the worker, given our situation. But we deeply appreciated his evenhandedness and honorable approach to things.

Somewhere in the middle of all of this, my brother Johnny came to Denver for a visit (from California). I'm sure he must have been at least vaguely aware of the bleakness of our situation, but I don't think we talked about it much. Johnny was a guy who liked to smell the roses even where there weren't any, and his way of cheering you up wasn't to analyze the situation or try to treat what ailed you with pills or palliatives (okay, maybe a glass of wine) or clever counsel. It was to make you see the lighter side. It was to make you laugh. He just did his thing and you felt better for being around him. To be Johnny was to be the medicine.

Johnny liked movies too, and one afternoon, we all – kids included – decided to go see one. Sounded like fun, something I hadn't really had in a while, and I eagerly stepped out our front door to find a beautiful day and Johnny and the kids awaiting me, alongside our chauffeur (Lauren) and limo (our old, rundown car).

Life was still good. And, as if to confirm the joyous ride that life could be, there on the sidewalk in front of me lay the kids' skateboard, beckoning me to get on board and hang ten. (Or was that a surfing term?) Whatever the case, I'd never stepped on a skateboard in my life – only fretted over the kids doing so. And now, newfound joy and abandon apparently overtaking my senses, I cast caution aside in favor of taking off on the skateboard like I'd been doing wheelies all my life (or was that a motorcycle term?). How hard could it really be for a 48-year-old woman with a fairly decent sense of balance?

The next thing I knew I was parallel to the sky (note to self: *Ah, Colorado! Not a cloud in the sky!*), engaged in a frantic effort to somehow right myself so as not to land on my head. It wasn't a pretty landing and I could feel, and actually hear, the crunch of bones. Had anyone else heard them? As I sat in a heap on the sidewalk, I took stock of the situation. It was clear to me my leg was broken and that I had just effected, not just a graceless fall, but a complete change of trajectory for everyone. Alas, we would not be going to the movies that afternoon. Overall though, I was overcome with a sense of gratitude that I hadn't come down on my head.

Pre-occupied as everyone was getting into the car, no one actually caught sight of my circus act, and now seeing me unmoving on the sidewalk, Lauren and the kids decided I was "just being funny". I can be funny, but I'm not *that* funny. "Come on, Mom!" said the kids. "Hurry up!" But there was something in our common DNA that allowed Johnny to instantly read his sister's facial expression, or lack of one. "Your mother's hurt," he said.

Hours later, I was prostrate on the couch, wearing a splint until the swelling could go down enough to cast the leg. The doctors had prescribed ankle surgery (I had suffered a complete fracture of the fibula and a number of fractured ankle bones), but given my previous adverse reactions to epidurals, even an assembly of five solicitous doctors and nurses could do nothing to convince me to go along with the idea. Instead, they eventually made the cast nice and tight and cautioned me that my ankle would henceforth serve as an effective weight barometer.

Needless to say, no more skateboards for this middle-aged mother.

I spent that first night on the couch poaching in a broth of gratitude, shock and a certain amount of pain, and wondering offhandedly what Louise Hay, author of "Heal Your Life", had to say about the deeper meanings of breaking a leg.[2] I chanted under my breath a good part of that sleepless night.

Days went by, weeks went by. The couch and I were best friends by then, and my oldest daughter was starting to tire of making trips to the Italian deli for fresh mozzarella. But I was starting to get back into life again too. I wrote a script during the latter part of my recovery, though I can't say it was one of my best. And I continued to communicate with Kim and deal with whatever faced us. Which, at this point, was mostly the afore-mentioned lawsuits.

I had (and have) many lovely friends, as does Kim, though looking back, I can see that I found it hard to share my deepest concerns with them. From a logical point of view, I knew that the act of dissecting the wound was not the strategy that would heal me. In fact, simply carving my troubles into smaller pieces only seemed to multiply the pain. That being the case, I had little desire to rehash the tale, talk about the minutiae, or analyze ad infinitum the things that were assailing me. I had one viable choice: to move forward, albeit with the help of crutches.

As for Kim, take that inclination of mine (of keeping things close to your chest) and multiply it by – well, at least two. But that didn't mean we didn't need or appreciate the comfort, friendship and understanding of those around us – especially given the hostile environment we'd been dealing with for so long. In fact, it gave us courage and raised our spirits to receive a word of comfort or hope –

or flowers! – from a friend. And, as said, we both had great friends. Most noteworthy of all during this time period, Kim had her best friend, Anna, and I had my husband and best friend, Lauren.

There were also the occasional off-kilter moments involving people who didn't seem to fathom the implications of what was happening to us. One screenwriting friend for whom I had the greatest esteem but who had little emotional room for my predicament, showed up at our door after I broke my leg, carrying a plate of homemade cookies. The cookies were a well-chosen gesture, but her words of comfort fell painfully short. "How's that leg?" she said, as she took a seat next to me on the couch. Not waiting for an answer, she added, as if there were continuity in the thought, "Sure glad I didn't invest in your movie!"

Whatever she had to say to me after that became a distortion of words, a grating and unwelcome sound in my ear. Well-intended as she might have been, and as much as I truly loved her, I felt only relief when she left.

Sure glad I never asked her to invest in my movie.

By now, I was doing pretty well on crutches, and good thing too, as my court date with the lumber company (the one with whom I'd signed a personal guarantee) was coming up.

The first thing the judge tells you when you're representing yourself is that going *pro se* is not such a hot idea (or, at least, I assume they say that to others, and not just to me). In any event, I certainly knew it wasn't a good idea, but I didn't have the luxury of being able to hire an attorney. The lumber company attorney was there, however, looking confident and well-prepared.

The judge spoke into his microphone as he began recording the session, duly noting that the defendant "*appears* to have a broken leg." It had not occurred to me until then that my cast and crutches might be perceived as a means to evoke sympathy from the court. This was far from being the case, but I wasn't there to defend my honor – only my circumstances – so I wisely held my tongue.

The attorney for the lumber company made his case, after which I spoke (nervously), explaining where things were at and why they had come to this. In the end, I asked for more time. The judge agreed. Perhaps he knew there was little point in doing otherwise, as I plainly was not in a position to make restitution to the lumber company at this point in time. I thanked the court, shook the attorney's hand, and hobbled out of the building.

———

One day, on the road to healing but still wearing a cast, I happened to glance at the cover of an entertainment magazine that had come in the mail. On the front cover, an upcoming movie was being featured – the very one that I feared might have been, at the least, inspired by one of the scripts we had (way back when) sent to a production company through Jake-the intermediary. We had since found out some things about the production company that potentially tied it to Denver and to our script, leaving me with an emptiness in the pit of my stomach and a feeling of having been personally violated. Nevertheless, I really wasn't sure I wanted to dig any deeper into the whole, potentially ugly, mess. I doubted that Kim wanted to either.

And anyway, you can't copyright a title, or an idea or concept, for that matter. The truth is, they really *are* fair play. There are many movies that share the same name, and there are many stories out there based on the same basic concept, i.e., boy meets girl, boy loses girl, boy wins girl back again. This is as it should be. Otherwise, the scope of any writer's turf would be pretty limited.

So, all you can really do when someone comes up with an idea that sounds a lot like yours is assume that there exists a collective consciousness that can give rise to simultaneous ideas (which there is). Beyond that, imitation being the sincerest form of flattery, you can feel flattered. But the only thing you can legally defend in a court of law is the execution of a concept, i.e., how much similarity there is in how your story and theirs play out. In this case, that comparison had yet to be made. And even if everything ended up pointing to a great injustice, the question was this: did Kim and I have the energy or the means to fight yet another legal battle – especially one that required money we didn't have?

Regarding the movie in question, my first agent, Diane, would later say to me that when it came out, she had asked herself *if Pam had sold her screenplay*. But, as she would also counsel, *you really don't want to be known in the industry as a litigious individual. People won't want to work with you*. Which kind of made me laugh, given our situation. Anyway, I'm not a litigious person. I just don't like the idea that the big guy can take advantage of the little guy just because he's bigger and wealthier, or more popular and well-known. It's called bullying, and it's no nicer when it happens in Hollywood than when it happens in school or on the street.

For now, however, there was only one thing on my mind. Being able to make it up the stairs on my rear end and into the bathtub, leg propped on the edge of the tub. Movies be damned! My kingdom for a bath!

1 - Answer: Winston Churchill

2 - Here's what I later read: *Fear of the future*.

WHEN THE GOING GETS TOUGH
Personal Bankruptcy

Early Sept. 1996 – *We've fought the idea – some might say the inevitable – for months, and there's no getting around it anymore. Pressure is building from all sides, requiring us to act. We have no recourse but to declare personal bankruptcy.*

On the lighter side of things, as I was pondering my fate, some young cashier at the grocery store was griping at me (in an effort to be friendly) that he lived from paycheck to paycheck, and that whoever invented money should be drawn and quartered. I felt his pain – in fact, his pain is still sending electric shocks throughout my body – but then I reminded him that, if we didn't have money, we'd be bartering with chickens, and he'd be griping that he didn't have enough of those or that they never laid him a golden egg. "Yeah," he agreed. "You're right." Standing on the fodder of common ground, we locked eyes and nodded at each other. I picked up my meager groceries, said goodbye and good luck, and walked out the door, still painfully aware that, whether cash or free-range chickens, Kim and I could sure use a few.

It should be said that neither Kim, nor I, thought lightly of the idea of declaring bankruptcy, personal or otherwise. In fact, the whole idea was somewhat foreign to our thinking, and certainly not something we had ever envisioned going through, regardless of the circumstances. All along, we had only wanted to make things work out for everyone, understanding that bankruptcy would effectively be the end of everything (of everything *A Bucket of Paint*). But, in the face of lawsuits breathing down our necks from all quarters, we found ourselves in a corner with no other way out.

We had tried to explain to those who had threatened us with lawsuits that, if we had to legally defend ourselves and forced to declare bankruptcy, there would be no financial restitution for anyone. The truth is, we had no money left to speak of. And, as we all know, try as you might, you can't get blood out of a turnip. The only hope for us and our creditors lay in continuing the quest to breathe new life into *A Bucket of Paint*. And, as long as there was still hope, we were game to keep trying.

But frustration was justifiably high, and although people certainly yearned for financial restitution, some seemed to yearn even more for personal payback. Lawsuits notwithstanding, our faith in Nico's ability to save the project was all but gone. It was getting time to call it a day. By all accounts, it had been a long one and surely no one could say we had given up easily.

We decided to declare personal bankruptcy, but to wait on corporate as long as we possibly could on the infinitesimal chance that Nico would still come through.

Given her legal background and contacts, Kim took on the task of finding us a reasonably-priced bankruptcy attorney with a solid reputation and found us the perfect person in Jeanne, a smart, experienced and understanding attorney, highly thought-of by her peers. We were grateful when Jeanne agreed to take our case, as this certainly wasn't your run-of-the-mill bankruptcy. Lauren (my husband) would have to be included in my personal bankruptcy as it would by necessity factor in any assets that carried both of our names – which is to say, everything.

As anyone knows who's ever declared personal bankruptcy, things change afterward, both for the better and for the worse. On the plus side, we would be able to put an end to the threats, harassment, and financial lawsuits that plagued us, and to some degree (but not completely) let go of the dead-weight of our pretty much defunct project, all of which would come as a huge relief. Best of all, the guy who rode his motorcycle by my house shouting obscenities at me would have to cease and desist.

On the negative side, we would have to relinquish pretty much anything of value that we owned. Whether we would be able to keep our homes would depend on the amount of equity we had in them. At the time, if one's equity was appraised any higher than $30,000, the house would have to be sold and the equity used to pay off creditors. Fortunately, at the end of the day, Kim and I were able to hold onto our homes. An independent appraisal estimated the equity in our home (Lauren's and mine) to be not less, not more, but exactly $30,000. Commented the judge," Well, that's convenient!" (or words to that effect). Indeed, it was convenient. But other than putting my prayers out to the Universe, I had nothing to do with influencing the outcome. I was deeply grateful though. Our home – even with two mortgages – was all we had going into the future.

Kim's and my (and Lauren's) credit scores, which had been excellent going into the project, would now take a nose dive – not that it mattered much at this point. Jeanne also advised us that our bankruptcies would continue to show up on our credit reports for ten years. However, there was a glimmer of good news! If at any point either one of us needed to buy a vehicle, there were dealerships that would oblige, regardless of our credit! And there was more good news! Credit card companies wanted our business, as we would soon discover when gold and platinum credit card applications began overloading our mailboxes. (Guess they figure you won't be able to get out of it this time.)

All facetiousness aside, there's no denying that the relief we felt was enormous. As was the pain of knowing it was pretty much over and that no one would be paid his or her due – that is, unless Nico performed a last-minute miracle. We would keep trying, but there would most likely be no film. No perfect ending to our dream. At least not now, and not as we had envisioned it.

As Bob (our business advisor) would say to me in an attempt to pave the way for what was to come, "...you'll probably want to chop off all your fingers before you ever write again." The point being, how could I ever allow my fingers to craft words on paper again when the end result had been so disastrous? I would have to be patient with myself. I would have to give it time. I understood Bob's point and valued the concern with which he expressed it. But writing was not just a passion for me, it was a necessity, part of what kept me going in life. To stop writing, even as part of some overall healing process, was not my way. And, besides, our travails had little to do with my writing, other than the fact that my writing supplied us with a project, hope, momentum, and trajectory. In other words, my writing set us on our way. But the difficulties we experienced along the way were the result of a host of other factors.

And so we went through the personal bankruptcy process, filling out quantities of paperwork – the sum of our financial lives, if you will. Creditors, without exception, had to be written off, even those we knew would never be of a mind to pursue us – such as my brother and sister-in-law and other supportive friends who had been development investors. No exceptions. That was the rule, and Jeanne advised our creditors of the situation accordingly. From this point forward, no one would have a legal right to pursue us – at least, personally.

On September 5th, we drafted a letter to our investors, reiterating the situation on a more personal level from our production company.

Here's that letter:

> September 5, 1996
>
> Dear Investor:
>
> As you may already have been apprised by notice from their legal counsel, both Pamela Nelson and Kimberly Ricotta have been compelled to file for individual Chapter 7 bankruptcy due to the impossibility of their personal situations pursuant to the misrepresentation by and subsequent default of ██████'s production investor.
>
> We can appreciate how long all of you have waited and hoped for a positive outcome to the ██████ project. We would like you to know, however, that we have relentlessly made efforts on behalf of the project during the course of the last nine months and that hope still exists that financing will be secured. Despite the severity of the corporation's financial circumstances, Shoe In The Road Productions, Inc. has not filed for bankruptcy at this time in order to allow this hope to play itself out on everyone's behalf. This is not to say that there are not complications involved. Nevertheless, our personal hopes for the project are real enough to merit some mention in this letter.
>
> We will notify you if, and when, the specifics of ██████'s financing are worked out. In the meantime, we thank you for the support you have given this project.
>
> Sincerely,
>
> SHOE IN THE ROAD PRODUCTIONS, INC.

It was starting to feel painfully obvious that no one was going to blow the trumpets and come to the rescue of a film whose producers had just resorted to personal bankruptcy. And yet, Nico felt there was still a chance. Better than a chance! (Think of all the Mondays ahead!) Mostly so we could tell ourselves we had left no stone unturned, we decided to drag our feet a while before declaring corporate bankruptcy.

Having now been informed of the latest turn of events. my parents, who lived only five minutes away from us (me, Lauren and family), came by to see how we were holding up. Being someone who relied heavily on baking to express her deeper emotions, my mother brought with her what was left of a German chocolate cake (the part my father hadn't already eaten). That was our family motto, after all:

When the going gets tough, the tough raid the pantry! I'm only half-joking, as I do have to credit southern-style strawberry shortcake, apple cobbler, and crème caramel for seeing me through some rough moments in life. But, in this instance, half a German chocolate, even with all that gloriously bad-for-you frosting on top, wasn't going to do the trick.

My parents stayed only long enough to assure themselves that we were essentially okay. We were, though we could have used a new washing machine, ours having broken down, compelling me to hole up at the laundromat for the good part of every Saturday. (This would go on until I suddenly had an epiphany between loads, which was that our Montgomery Ward's credit card had not been written off in bankruptcy, since we had never used it. *Hello!* Much as we didn't want to rack up any more debt, we purchased that new washer faster than you can say, *Get me out of this effing laundromat!*).

My father offered to pay for an attorney, but the last thing I wanted was to embroil my parents in our financial difficulties. It was sweet of him, but accepting his offer would have only made things harder on me emotionally, and so – with gratitude – we declined.

Mom's parting words that day surprised me, and I've never forgotten them. She said, "Well, honey, for what it's worth, I would never have had the courage to do what you did." Having suffered through the Depression and having prematurely lost her father at a time when his income was badly needed to sustain their large family, Mom was the epitome of frugality and good money sense and was always quick to point out her children's erring financial ways. But she was also never one to hit you when you were down. I closed the door behind them and wept.

STAYING ALIVE
From La-la Land to A Federation of the World

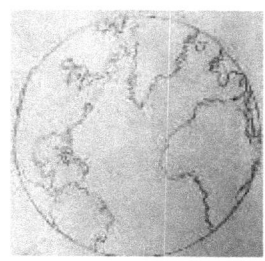

September 1996 *– I've been scrambling to find a job, but really cannot bear to have it be something (that feels) trivial. My good job-hunting fortune takes me to an interview with a very interesting older couple who have visions of transforming the world. Together, they have worked since the end of World War II to create and foster a political structure that would unite the countries of the world under a Federation. They are both pacifists and visionaries, and have also been working on ways to reverse carbon dioxide emissions and resulting climate change (for which the general public has yet to accept human-generated acceleration). We talk and they hire me, asking me if I'm free to go to Zaragoza, Spain in barely two weeks' time. I'll have to end my physical therapy (broken leg-related) prematurely, but I'm totally game to go, and eager to explore new horizons and maybe even contribute in some way to the planet's welfare. It's not movie-making, but as a pacifist myself, the idea definitely appeals to some significant side of me.*

I try not to limp as I walk out of the office.

Kim, also, was looking for a job. Referred by our bankruptcy attorney, she landed work at a law firm in early November. Things were pretty tough from a money (or lack thereof) point of view for both of us (and, needless to say for my husband, Lauren), where they would remain into our gainful employment and well beyond. Kim's mother and sister pitched in and bought her clothes to wear on the job hunt and then, subsequently, to wear on the job. Coming home after a long day's work, it wasn't unusual for Kim to find that they had stocked her refrigerator while she was away, wanting to make sure she had enough to eat. (Now, that's a good Italian family for you!)

All I wanted in the world was for my husband to give up his second job painting houses. Lauren is good, strong Scandinavian stock (or so I used to tease him), but the truth is, even a good, strong Scandinavian will wear out after climbing too many ladders, swatting away too many wasps, and scraping and spray-painting too many peeling houses as a second job. I prayed the day would come when we could retire the painting jersey but, for now, that day wasn't quite around the corner.

Prior to our employment, Kim and I were open to whatever gigs we could find to earn a little extra cash. For example, we were hired through an acquaintance of Kim's to be two of a handful of bit players (no audible dialogue) in a video for a well-known high-end brand of purses. We were put up at a hotel in Colorado Springs where we stayed up late laughing at our immediate situation (the gig) and watching whatever free movie was on t.v. – something a little too violent for both of us, as we remember, so we finally opted for sleep. The next morning, we showed up early at the Cheyenne Mountain Inn for the all-day shoot.

Did we feel humbled by our fall from feature film producers to video extras for fancy purses? Not really. We were just happy to be earning some money. And, strangely – maybe because it was a welcome respite from unemployment, or maybe because the whole thing seemed crazy and convoluted and a strange detour from what we had envisioned for our futures – it was a bit of unanticipated fun.

Given her background, Kim was a natural, but even I was complimented on my unexpected ability to pretend to be making small talk. Who knew. Said the kind Director to the acting potential incarnate that was (not) I, "Not everyone can do that." Maybe so, but I won't be doing it again soon.

In the meantime, *A Bucket of Paint* was still a part of our psyche and of our daily lives, often impinging on the reality that was closer at hand, i.e., our jobs. Despite personal bankruptcy (corporate had yet to be filed), dealing with disgruntled people and other related matters was still – though gradually dissipating – at least, a thrice-weekly affair. Kim and I took turns returning calls in our spare time, an unpleasant task, but one we had a personal responsibility not to ignore.

So, never mind that I was trying to get ready for an international conference in a foreign country, when it was my turn, it was my turn. And now I had to find a moment to call back a member of the cast re the Helix Hotel fiasco. There was nothing to be done about any of it, and the only purpose of my call-back was to let her get things off her chest. She deserved that, and it had to be faced. On break, I picked up the phone and dialed the number. There was that "F" word again and, this time, not out of my mouth, but from someone who felt just as justified to use it as I had when I lost my cool over the Viper. When the conversation was over, I hung up the phone and went back to what I was doing, but the echo of that call rang in my ears and stayed with me a good, long time.

We were still dealing with Nico too, but less and less, and certainly with less-than-zero hopefulness. Eventually, he faded into thin air like the long-lasting, but elusive bubble that he was, Candi floating alongside him. Or maybe she popped first. At any rate, we hardly noticed the departure from our lives of two people who had taken us for a painful and prolonged ride to nowhere. Well, nowhere pleasant.

Among other unpleasant tasks, checking the mailbox, a once happy affair, was no longer the hopeful highlight of the day that it had once been. Kim and I now made our way through the mail as if compelled to sort through a pile of hazardous waste material. Latex gloves wouldn't have been inappropriate. On my end, letters began arriving from a particular development investor who needed to vent. His words were sad more than they were accusatory, but the underlying message was that he needed his money back and only the restitution of his investment would make things right for him again. This was, of course, an impossible request, and though his appeals tugged at my heart, I had no ready fix for his suffering.

―――

So the next thing I knew, I was at the airport, on my way to Zaragoza, alongside my two co-workers. I knew very little about them, apart from the fact that they often holed up together overnight in the supply closet. Other than that, I can only say that he was British and in charge of the database, she was soft-spoken, and they seemed to exist in their own double bubble – ergo, we saw no reason to hook up on the airplane.

My boss, Albert, was a maverick. So was his wife, Eleanor. She was strong and capable and beautiful even in her seventies. Unfortunately, she was compelled by circumstances to remain in Colorado. I was disappointed. In the short time I had known her, I had grown to like her and to look forward to our brief morning chats. Her backstory was intriguing. Her opinions were strong and riveting. She was knowledgeable. I thought of her as something of a mentor. Together, she and her husband were a force to be reckoned with – a force for change and the betterment of conditions on our planet – against the backdrop of a world that wasn't quite ready for their political and environmental visions.

And she was interested in film too. We talked about possibilities related to her political passions. (I'm sad to say, she did not live too much longer – and certainly not long enough to see her visions for the world come true.)

While my time in Zaragoza might, at first blush, seem to be a detour from our ongoing saga, it really isn't. I'll tie it together.

Hundreds of delegates were expected for the conference, the aim of which, generally stated, was to promote the idea and implementation of a world federation. Many of these delegates came from Third World countries. In the interest of not leaving sincere delegates out of the equation, Albert had helped pay travel expenses for many who needed it, and waived fees for many others. Despite the help, the conference was thwarted from the get-go by governmental opposition, and only a vastly reduced number were able to make it – which was just as well, as political issues had already forced the conference to a much smaller venue.

Albert had been promoting the idea of a world currency as an ideal for the future, but the message was not as clear as it should have been and caused a great deal of confusion among delegates, especially certain individuals from Zaire (the Democratic Republic of the Congo). A contingency of these individuals (the Zairian mafia, as best we could figure) believed that money was there for the taking (specifically, from Albert). Not world peace, but extortion, became their primary focus. And, because I spoke French, I was called upon as the interpreter for the whole nasty mess. It wasn't quite as fun interpreting for extortionists as it was for the governmental representatives from Togo, but it was certainly helpful to me in expanding my French vocabulary.

Add a mix of undercover CIA, being followed wherever we went, and even being physically harassed, and you can see that my trip to Zaragoza wasn't what the travel agents tell you it's going to be. Not eager to stick around for all the excitement, my British co-worker up and quit early on, taking off for parts unknown with his closet-buddy in tow. I bid them adieu, envying them their freedom from what was starting to become a truly unsettling scenario.

As the weight of the conference gone-awry came down on Albert, and as people fell to the wayside of an increasingly ugly situation, my own determination to stay and support intensified. I made up my mind to be there for Albert, come what may. Believe me, he could hold his own without my help, but that wasn't the point. The point was, our film ordeal had taught me the kind of person I wanted to be. I wanted to be the one you could count on at a crucial moment. The one who wouldn't jump ship. In short, I wanted Albert (or any other friend or well-intentioned employer) to be able to count on me when things got bad. I knew how much it meant to have someone's unwavering support when the chips were down.

I made some friends in the process — friends who, regardless of distance and opposing life trajectories, will always remain in my heart. Real friends, the ones who rise to the occasion during hard times, are worth their weight in gold. *A Bucket of Paint* had taught me that too. Well, maybe not taught me — but certainly gone a long way toward reminding me.

MAY IT PLEASE THE COURT
Corporate Bankruptcy

July 1997 *– Well, it's been a long foot-drag and our toes are hurting, but our corporate bankruptcy hearing is finally happening. It's been an arduous journey from our days of innocence to this unexpected finale. The movie actually did "go south", as my brother Gary once mused that it might. Back then, we never thought it possible. Well, not probable, anyway. Hard to say how we're feeling about things. Buffeted by the winds of change, for sure – but, what the heck, still standing. It helps that we've already mourned the project, maybe not fully, but enough to ease our way into this final step.*

Jeanne, our attorney, tells us we're unusual. By the time they've filed for corporate bankruptcy, she says, most business partners are pointing the finger at each other. We've definitely experienced that phenomenon from others in the months leading up to today, but not when it comes to each other. We remain steadfast in our friendship and in our respect for each other.

In all the tumult, we haven't had a moment to think about the future, but the line between the past and the future is about to be drawn. A Bucket of Paint will soon be relegated to the world of dreams – a memory, ephemeral, a thing of the past. Kim and I will need some time to recuperate from our ordeal before we plunge headlong into the future, whatever that might look like. In the interim, a vacation would be nice. Kim's dreaming of a tropical island. Me, I'm headed to Malta, glass of fine wine in hand. But only in my mind. Vacations cost money, and for now, a long night's sleep will have to do. Oh, and maybe a glass of that $5.00-a-bottle Chianti.

We wanted to laugh when we saw the tally, except that it wasn't funny. Or, rather, it was the kind of funny that can only be expressed at an appropriate moment, i.e., twenty years later – and even then, only in the form of a muffled guffaw, and not an all-out laugh.

But there it was before our eyes, translated into dollars and cents in case we didn't already have a clue (bankruptcy has a way of cutting to the chase). In sum total, here was *Shoe in the Road*'s final score going into bankruptcy:

Total assets: $35
Total liabilities: $1,056,673.09

Now, granted, we didn't actually owe $1,056,673.09, but to be on the safe side, we needed to include items that – while not considered actual debts – could someday turn around and bite us. As for our assets, Kim and I could only wonder how we had managed to hold on to $35.

We showed up for court ready to get it over with. I don't remember being in a bad mood that morning – just feeling like I'd been tasered long and hard and now had to pick myself up off the sidewalk, shake it off, and keep on going. But there was also something in the air – a coolness, a crispness, a sunny kind of hopefulness. The war was finally over! The city had been flattened, but the occupiers were leaving town. We wouldn't have to look over our shoulders anymore. Maybe now we could start to rebuild our lives instead of merely defending them.

So – not so weirdly, I guess – what we felt that morning was a mixture of apprehension and joy, though in the scheme of things, joy was still an acorn, and apprehension was a massive, towering oak tree.

Jeanne (our attorney), who was already in the building, greeted us warmly, and quickly apprised us of what to expect. Earlier, we had received a letter from her, informing us that the bankruptcy trustee intended to auction off the script (*A Bucket of Paint*) to help pay off creditors. But that turned out to be pretty much a no-go, given the fact that the DGA already had a secured lien against the motion picture. Now, however, there was a new turn of events. Ron, who, along with other creditors, would have a chance to have his say in court, was apparently planning to petition the court to have my scripts (among them, the ones for which he had put together budget top sheets and which had been sent to those anonymous producers) consigned to him, as reparation for monies owed and pain inflicted. It's not as if I felt I were going to be selling scripts all over town (I wasn't that naïve anymore), but still! – handing over my babies would not be easy, and were that to be the court's judgment, my plan was to traverse the distance between me and Ron in a single leap, latch onto his ankles, and be dragged from the court kicking and screaming.

Jeanne did her best to put our minds at ease. As we conferred with her prior to the hearing in what we thought to be privacy, the doors to the room quietly opened and in slid Ron. We all nodded at each other, but Kim and I felt an instant discomfort, especially as he moved in closer. After all, we were trying to discuss private matters with our attorney. It was totally unnerving.

At long last, we were invited into the courtroom and the proceedings began.

Somewhere in all of it, Ron stepped up to the podium to make his case to the court. At some level, we weren't too surprised at Ron's initiative in the matter, though we certainly hadn't anticipated it. There was something almost pitiable in his voice, and we couldn't help feeling sorry for him. Nevertheless, I was still ready to make the leap if he tried to walk out of the courtroom with my screenplays.

To be honest, however, we didn't feel *that* sorry for him. Months ago, when lawsuits were filing in, Kim and I had made a list of our grievances toward him just for the record, which ran two full typewritten pages in length. We were astounded, both by the magnitude of the list itself, and even more so, by our own lack of decisive action when confronted with each perceived wrong. *Why hadn't we corrected the situation early on*, we asked ourselves, *when there was still a chance to get back on track*? After all, Ron was experienced and had all the makings of an efficient Line Producer. That failing, *why didn't we reclaim our project?*

Nigel was right. It's important to speak up, especially at the crucial moment. Instead, here we were in bankruptcy court, reflecting on a useless list of grievances against Ron when, in fact, the biggest grievance we had was with ourselves for not standing up with all the fierce determination we had once mustered on behalf of our film, and reclaiming control over our project.

Gloria took her turn at the podium. Our relationship with her had been more reserved recently, but she had been our Co-Producer and friend and worked and laughed alongside us. Now, as she stood before the court and made her plea for reparations, we looked on with a sense of sadness, though we understood that it was just a case of business being business. Nothing more, nothing less. And nothing personal. And, naturally, she wanted it stated for the record – she was not responsible for *A Bucket of Paint*'s demise. And she wasn't.

Ron's request was denied and my screenplays were to remain my property. And if, one day, Kim and I wanted to do something with them, we'd cross that bridge (wearing all the proper protective gear) when we came to it. But, frankly, that was the last thing on our minds. Right now all we wanted to do was shake our attorney's hand, leave the building, and breathe that long repressed sigh of relief.

We stood outside the courthouse, looked at each other and smiled. One of those mixed feelings kind of smile, but a smile nonetheless.

It was finally over.

AFTERSHOCK
Dealing with Internal Injuries

August 1997 *– Corporate bankruptcy may finally be over and the project defunct, but Kim and I still have things to deal with – mostly having to do with sorting out our lives. We know we've lost a big battle, but we're determined not to give up on ourselves or our aspirations for the future. We decide to meet weekly, even if it's just to talk, or sometimes commiserate (come on – just a little?) over a cup of coffee. We're beginning to realize the extent of our injuries, which are primarily psychic in nature. We can't let ourselves be defeated, but we have to be patient with ourselves too. (As Bob intimated, healing takes time.) We try to find reasons to laugh. We still cry on a frequent basis. It's just a fact of life, and probably a normal part of recovery.*

People have asked why we didn't turn around and sue Candi for breach of contract. The short answer is that there would have been no point in it. Lawsuits are a pain in the you-know-what and a terrible way to spend your time. Still, had she been hoarding millions under her mattress, we might have considered the possibility. Did we hate her for what she put us through? No. What's the point in that? Besides, it's not in our nature. If anything, we felt sorry for the sad state of affairs that seemed to be her life and could only hope she'd find a way to turn things around for herself. That being said, we obviously didn't take her default lightly, nor did we take lightly the painful inconvenience and financial injury that her default had caused to *A Bucket of Paint's* cast and crew, and to ourselves and my family.

Anyway, it should never have come to Candi. Had we handled things properly when she walked in that door that fateful day, we would have had no use for her. Even more accurately, had we handled things properly, she might never have walked in the door. We wouldn't have moved forward until the production money was in the bank. Contracts with the actors would have honored our original investor's right to recoupment plus a percentage from first monies. The need for extraneous funds would have been a non-issue. But, even in the face of such an entanglement, Kim and I should have held fast to our original investor, even if it meant rocking the Ron-boat, even if it meant taking the chance of losing certain actors in the process, even if it meant having to seriously revise or reduce the budget. At least we would have had a movie.

So, there you have it. In the end, there was no point in suing anyone because a) there was no money to be gained by it; and b) we ourselves were to blame for making bad decisions[1] while not taking full charge of our film.

Though many people were financially injured through the demise of *A Bucket of Paint*, Kim and I had thrown good money after bad trying to keep things alive, and still ended up in bankruptcy. Unlike others, including Ron, we hadn't benefited from being on the payroll and didn't receive a weekly check (other than a one-time check to reimburse ourselves for some expenses, in the vicinity of $350). The more than $300,000 that we had raised for development of the film (and then to keep it going because of our premature and ill-fated start), was never spent to pay ourselves. The truth is, fees for any cast and crew should not have come due, or been paid, until the money to make the movie (the production money) was in the bank. Yes, we got up and running prematurely and people still had to be paid, but we still didn't feel it proper to inject salaries for ourselves into a premature payroll.

Our attorney pointed out this "oversight" (her word) during the filing of our bankruptcy. After listing all of *Shoe in the Road*'s creditors, she pointed out that we needed to amend the paperwork.

"Why?" we asked.

"Because you didn't put in a claim for yourselves. You're owed wages just as much as anyone else."

It had never occurred to us to list ourselves. Not that it ultimately would have made any difference.

But financial injuries were the least of what ailed us as we wrapped up corporate bankruptcy. By far, the deeper injuries were internal. For months, beginning with personal bankruptcy, Kim and I had walked around in a daze, lacking emotional equilibrium. It wasn't that our film was going down. We could have dealt with that. You win some, you lose some, and sometimes it hurts like hell. But, as my mother, who had picked up (and never let go of) a favorite word in Egypt, would have said, "Malish" – rough translation, *don't worry about it*. Life – the show – must go on.

Had we been able to properly analyze our feelings at the time, it would have been clear to us that our psychic injuries were two-fold. First, as two people who had looked forward to contributing to the joy and prosperity of others, the fact that we had caused them pain instead was hard for us to bear. Secondly, having been battered by others for so long – particularly by people who had at one time treated us as friends – was beyond perplexing. In fact, it was deeply disorienting. I kept asking myself rhetorical questions like, "Weren't we the same people the day before things fell apart that we are today?" (Circumstances had changed. We hadn't. So why were people treating us as if we were less than we were yesterday?) Most of all, the lack of predictability, or consistency, in people I thought I knew, shook me to the core, though as I later came to understand, sometimes it's not that people change, it's that the mask falls off.

I began having nightmares around this theme. So did Kim.

Then there was the fact that Candi and Nico, from all evidence, had strung us along for so long. What did this say about us? And were they laughing at us in their private moments? Was everyone?

The upshot was that I, who had always loved people and found it hard to see anything but good in them, temporarily lost my faith in humanity. Buddhists aren't supposed to do that! Oh, well... I guess they're human too. Kim suffered from some of the same – for her, it was a question of trust. Who could you really trust in life? And, at the heart of our malady was this sense of being an untouchable, an unlikeable, an undeserving.

From Kim:
One day, around the time of our bankruptcy, I was downtown, probably job searching, when I stepped into an elevator. As the door closed, a person in the not-so-crowded compartment smiled at me and said, "Hi". I didn't see it coming, but I burst into tears. A simple greeting by this kind stranger had overwhelmed me. My bizarre reaction was no doubt unsettling to those stuck in the compartment with me, and I was certain they'd all make a hasty escape on the next floor. Apparently, I had lost so much trust in people, I momentarily forgot how to respond to cordial-speak. It's always surprising how something out of the blue can hit you like an emotional steam engine.

I myself had a similar experience. Except that it wasn't in an elevator and the words were slightly different. My unsuspecting greeter happened to say, "How are you?"

(I don't think people realize how profound a question that is. Try saying it as if you really mean it, as if you really care, sometime. Better yet, mean it and care. You might be surprised at the responses you'll get.)

Thankfully, my practice (which remained consistent and, in fact, a real imperative) gave me the strength to endure and, eventually, to see the good in people again. We're all just human, after all, possessing infinite potential no matter what our outer shell. But face it, which one of us would run into a burning building to save a child? My husband would, and has (though, as it turned out, there was no child inside). Which one of us would have ceded our place on that last lifeboat, had we been passengers on the Titanic? My husband would have. Which one of us would give our last cookie to a hungry spouse? Not him. He doesn't share cookies well. (But he might run into a burning building to save a box of cookies...!)

The point is, we really don't know how deep our strength and nobility run until they are tested. We like to think we are made of the right stuff, but we still have to believe in it, to hone it, and to call upon it when the crucial moment comes. Until then, our mettle exists in theory only.

At the same time, to be human is to be a work in progress. So, if we don't live up to the litmus test when we come face to face with it, or if others don't, we have to believe there's still hope for all of us. That's the conclusion I came to, and with time and prayer, this perspective helped me get past my emotional roadblock and see people again in the light of their humanity.

Though we sometimes made mistakes (okay, we made some colossal ones), we always strove to do the right thing. Consequently, we were always able to look at ourselves in the mirror and see two people we still liked and were proud of, even when it seemed that those around us saw us differently. In retrospect, of course, we wish we'd exercised better judgment, held on to our power with our last ounce of strength, and fully appreciated our ability to run the ball into the in-zone – or, as Kim would say, put the "biscuit in the basket".[2]

───

Nineteen-ninety-seven was an interesting year in another film-related way. On March 24th, prior to our official corporate bankruptcy (but with paperwork being prepared), the 69th Academy Awards took place. Kim and I couldn't help but watch them – why stop now? That year, *The English Patient* won Best Picture. What was interesting to us about that was that the film had suffered its own debacle around the same time we were suffering ours. The specifics, of course, weren't the same, but there were still some similarities – oh, except for the happy ending.

Here's the story, as told on IMDb (Internet Movie Database):

Originally, 20th Century Fox was to finance the film, but disputes arose between the studio and the producers over casting… After the producers refused to give in on a series of casting choices, Fox backed out of the film, and the project was uncertain just as production was about to begin. However, within a few weeks - during which the cast and crew stayed on in Italy without knowing if the film would be made - the film was picked up by Miramax.

Someone had come to the rescue, and the end result was an Oscar for Best Picture. Now, of course, *A Bucket of Paint* was not the genre of movie that would typically be nominated for Best Picture – we had no illusions about that, though we certainly believed our film would do well. But the story of *The English Patient's* rescue and, ultimately, its success at the Oscars, had a fairytale quality about it that was certainly appealing to us and elicited a mutual sigh.

There were other sigh-worthy moments (for us) taking place at the Oscars that year. Granted, Frances McDormand had only been loosely attached to our film when she opted out. Still, seeing her win Best Actress felt strangely close to home.

Mare Winningham was also nominated for Best Supporting Actress. We had only been around her a short time, but our memories of her were sweet. We rooted for her.

Most poignant of all was Michael Flatley and his troupe's Irish riverdance performance— so similar to the dancing that was going to be featured in *A Bucket of Paint* and that we had so looked forward to seeing on the big screen.

It was as if 1997 had been destined to be our year, but wasn't.

It took a few days, but we got over it. Sometimes you just have to say, *It wasn't meant to be.* I'm not really sure what that means, but in this case, I'm philosophically okay with it.

1 – Bad decisions are interesting things. Often, the only thing that separates a good decision from a bad one is not the soundness of the decision, but its outcome. Which also begs the question – what is the timeframe on outcome? Do ripple effects, both negative and positive, count? And, is it possible, as Buddhism teaches, to turn even the most virulent poison into medicine?

2 - Needless to say, Pam is a Broncos fan, while Kim roots for the Avalanche. (And, of course, come what may, we're both Rockies fans. You have no choice when you live in Denver.)

CATCHING FIREFLIES
The Oxygen Bra & Other Inspirations

April 1998– *What does one do after bankruptcy but try to rebuild one's life – at least, the financial side of one's life? At the same time, Kim and I can't deny, or even suppress, the creative urges that, stubborn as they are, still surge within us. That being said, we certainly don't want to (nor are we in a position to) take crazy chances, but short of that, and despite the pain that may still be lingering at a cellular level, we're game to give our inner voices a chance to have their say as they alert us to a creative inspiration or a new idea.*

The first inspiration we had after laying *A Bucket of Paint* to rest was for a book. Not a book about *A Bucket of Paint,* of course. That was just too.... well, fresh. No, this was a book about something a little more removed – the Federation of the World that Albert and Eleanor advocated and on behalf of which I now contributed my efforts as Office Manager and whatever else (almost any job I've ever had has consisted of a heavy dose of "whatever else").

Actually, the inspiration first manifested itself as a screenplay, for no better reason than because that's what I had been writing for so long. I wanted it to be a love story set in both the present and the future – inspired by, but certainly not based on real-life characters –

just a telling of the possibility of the countries of the world coming together as one, much in the same way that the United States had come together under a constitutional federal government, a prospect I found intriguing. It was also interesting to me that people found it easy to embrace the idea of a future federation of planets (i.e., *Star Trek*), but by and large were alarmed by the idea of a united Earth. I wanted people to think about it, just as I had been made to think about it. I called the screenplay, *Federation*. (Can't get any more on-the-nose than that.)

Kim and I had fantasies of producing the screenplay, but no desire to actually do it, as we weren't of a mind to try to raise even more millions than before (actually, we weren't of a mind to raise a single penny), nor were we up for the overall production process, which would have been daunting, to say the least. In short, *A Bucket of Paint* wasn't far enough behind us for us to be entertaining the idea of going at it again.

Other inspirations were coming from my affiliation with Albert and Eleanor, one of which had to do with the environment. As the Project Manager for the foundation that Eleanor had established with the aim of finding ways to bring down carbon dioxide levels and increase oxygen levels, I became completely engrossed in the subject matter. I did a lot of research on the subject – not that there was all that much information to be accessed at the time. Scientists, with rare exception, were not admitting to the reality of climate change, and only a handful of people were out there really trying to come up with solutions. Albert used to tear his hair out (he had some to spare) over the state of the environment, specifically what he considered to be irreversible climate change – irreversible, that is, unless humanity could quickly admit to the problem and come up with what would presumably have to be one or more radical solutions.

One day, he looked at me with those penetrating blue eyes and asked, "What do you say when you get frustrated?"

"Frustrated?

"Frustrated. Mad. Upset."

"When I get mad?"

"When you get mad."

"I don't know. Shit? Damn?"

He nodded pensively, then confessed, "I say oo-lee-la."

Oo-lee-la?

So now it was on the table. I said *shit* and *damn* in the face of life's little frustrations, while he tugged at his hair over climate change and said *oo-lee-la*.

I couldn't help but love him, and I say this without the least condescension, as he was a visionary and had the determination of a bull.

Anyway, the direct result of my being immersed in all this fuel for thought was an idea for another screenplay, which I tentatively entitled, O^2.

It was around this time that I got a phone call from an agent in California named David who had heard of me through my previous agent, Diane. (Diane and I had parted ways amicably for reasons I don't even remember, probably having to do with Kim's and I being immersed in producing *A Bucket of Paint*.) He expressed an interest in representing me, and I flew out to California to meet him for no other reason than that I wanted to look into his eyes. Being the window to the soul, eyes were particularly important to me, especially now. They were nice eyes, as it turns out, so I agreed to be his client. Presumably, my eyes were nice enough too, as he also agreed to be my new agent. Mission accomplished, I turned around and flew home.

Although I had pitched the O^2 screenplay to David, and shown him my treatment (lengthy synopsis), when I finally sat down to write the screenplay, I was keenly aware that it was not my best work. In fact, I was keenly aware that it was almost as bad as the first screenplay I had ever written. I had Kim read it and she basically concurred. Good partners are honest with you, you know. Much as the subject matter was interesting to me, I was not inspired to revise the screenplay. It became obvious to me that I wasn't ready to tell that story. Maybe some other day.

In the meantime, while David pitched the *Federation* screenplay to a couple of potential producers, Kim and I decided it would be a good idea to publish it as a book. We decided to call the book, *When the Moon Comes Over the Mountain*, though years later, we would make some changes to it, finally re-publishing it as *Federation: When the Moon Comes Over the Mountain, New Edition* in 2016.

We sent a copy of *When the Moon Comes Over the Mountain* to Bob and received a nice letter in return (excerpted below).

> Hello Pam + Kim
>
> What a lovely surprise for this gift from my past to arrive at my door some many weeks ago.
>
> Pam it is a delightful "first novel". Your phrasing is beautiful. Your strength of character, something each of us who have known you admire so much — access into your story from so many directions. Please keep it up through novels two and three and beyond.

(Hello Pam & Kim – What a lovely surprise for this gift from my past to arrive at my door some many weeks ago. Pam it is a delightful "first novel". Your phrasing is beautiful. Your strength of character, something each of us who have known you admire so much – bleeds into your story from so many directions. Please keep it up through novels two and three and beyond.)

It meant a lot to us to hear back from him.

Though O^2 was off the table for now, I still had a passion for the subject matter. After many discussions on the topic with Kim, she also developed a strong interest in the subject. Later, after Eleanor had sadly passed away and I myself had left the enterprise (the organization, not the spaceship), the foundation seemed to fall into a state of inactivity. Trying in some way to fill the gap, Kim and I decided to start a non-profit as a side project, with the idea of continuing to promote discussion around the subject. We called it, *The Foundation for Oxygen Research*. My brother, Craig, gave us the money to file the extensive paperwork required for a non-profit corporation.

Soon, we were official. But, while we were well-intended and did carry out some awareness campaigns, our stated objectives were just a little too ambitious for us at this point in our lives, given the commitment that a non-profit of this nature required. Eventually, we dissolved the corporation, content in the knowledge that we had done some measure of good along the way.

In conjunction with the Foundation, we had also come up with an idea for an item of clothing that tied into the whole O^2 concept (that oxygen levels were diminishing, affecting human health, and were potentially implicated in rising cancer rates). Our idea was to create a bra that featured, not only completely organic, non-toxic materials and no underwire, but also promoted an uninterrupted flow of oxygen to the breasts. (Oh, and be gluten-free. *Just kidding!*)

Stifle your laughter, please. I still want one.

As with the *Oxygen Bra*, ideas would come to us and we would spring on them like they were fireflies. But sometimes we forgot to punch holes in our glass jars and our fireflies quickly suffocated. Sometimes they just weren't happy in the jar, holes or no holes. And sometimes fireflies should just be admired and left alone to glow in the night.

I'm not sure which category the *Oxygen Bra* fit into, if any of the above, but we believed in it so solidly that we met with an attorney in an attempt to patent the idea. As it turned out, the only thing stopping us from obtaining the patent was lack of money. Like so many others with creative ideas who try to run with them, we quickly collided with the no-money road block. And that's pretty much where, after a certain amount of exhaustive leg work, we let the firefly lie.

So there you have it. Nobody today wears an *Oxygen Bra*. At least, not ours, and not that we know of.

———

While I was still employed with Albert, Kim and I were tasked (by Albert) with producing a documentary on the subject of environmental impacts on oxygen levels. We hired a director Kim knew, put together an outline for him, and had him film and include footage from the oxygen-related conference that Albert put on in another state (and at which I was one of the speakers). The documentary was to be used solely for educational purposes. A worthy cause, though not exactly up our alley (we weren't really documentarians). Still, it was satisfying to feel that we had finally gotten back on our chosen path, even in some small way.

At some point and after a lot of deliberation, Kim and I finally did meet with a well-respected attorney regarding that high concept, blockbuster-type movie that smacked so disturbingly of my screenplay, who compelled me to go see the movie at the theater so I could make a list of similarities. *Go see it? You go see it! I don't want to see it!* But I did go see it. And, dutifully, I made my notes. Brian, our attorney, read the script along with my notes, saw the movie, and told us he thought we had a good case, so much so that he was willing to take it on contingency (meaning that the attorney's payment is contingent upon there being recovery or reward in the case.) We would need to prove access (the means for the script to have made it into the other party's hands), but given the fact that the script had been well circulated, access might be viewed as a given, even if we couldn't prove it had been put directly into the potential offender's hands.

In the meantime, we had consulted with an attorney in California who came back with the same verdict and who also wanted to take the case on contingency.

There was one catch, though. We'd have to pay expenses, which the attorneys assured us they would try to keep at a minimum. But, Brian cautioned, the opposing party was obviously in a position to drag things out and bleed us dry – which would be really easy to do, given the fact that we'd already been hung out to dry some time ago.

Brian's idea was to file for an injunction on the video, a court order that compels a certain party to carry out, or refrain from carrying out, specifics acts – in this case, putting out the video. With an injunction in place, there could be no revenue from video sales or rentals until the matter was settled. Interesting idea.

Again, there was a catch. And the catch was this. I really didn't want my life to be about lawsuits. I'd had enough of them. At this point, I was more interested in changing my karma, if you will. More interested in making a cause to move on to greater things in the broadest possible sense. Kim was in total agreement. It was painful to both of us to feel like we'd been hit while we were down – maybe even more so for me as the writer of a screenplay I had put so much into (probably more than any other screenplay as it had required extensive research and personal interviews) – but as I told Kim, *Good thing that's not my only screenplay! Good thing that screenplay isn't my life!* And so, we decided, in the words of Donnie Brasco[1], to "Forget about it!"

Every once in a while, Kim would run into Brian downtown and he would remind her that the statute of limitations hadn't run out, but at that point, she would just smile as the elevator doors closed behind him. Who really wants life to be about the hurts of the past?

"Hon'in-myo!" exhort my like-minded friends. *From this moment on!* The point being that the present moment is the only vehicle by which to transform the sufferings of the past into the cause for present and future happiness. That word alone was, and still is, a source of great encouragement to me.

1 – The 1997 movie starring Al Pacino and Johnny Depp, directed by Mike Newell

LIFE GOES ON
Kim Finally Gets a Pedicure

Spring of 1999 – *Family and friends have never scorned or belittled our endeavors, but they have to secretly wonder – and even sometimes wonder out loud – what are Pam and Kim up to now? After all, we've been meeting every damn week toward some end or another for the past... well, a long, long time!*

We've never laid our feature film dream to rest, but it's idling, waiting for the right year, the right month, the right moment. Practically speaking, we have to keep on making a living. In the meantime, continuing to meet, to talk, to dream, and sometimes to stumble forward with some new idea, is all we can do, as we know full well that if we don't, the dream won't just stagnate – it will end.

But what is the dream made of now? Has it changed, after all we've been through? In many ways it has, and yet, in the most significant way, it hasn't. One day we want to make a feature film from start to finish. It doesn't really matter what. Low budget. Zero budget. Just something we can put our arms around, hold onto, and call our own.

After Albert's wife passed away, I stayed on for as long as I felt I could. But Albert and I had slightly different perspectives on a few things, and eventually, they came to a head. For example, Albert wanted to hold that year's conference in Iraq (this was just as bombs were starting to drop in Operation Desert Fox), despite the fact that the State Department now forbade Americans to enter the country.

Well, you could probably get into the country, but you couldn't come back to the U.S. without being arrested and/or paying a hefty fine – that's if you lived to try to get back home.

But Albert's concerns lay elsewhere. After all, he looked forward to a world in which the only ID you might need would identify you as a citizen of the world (we're not there yet by a long shot, but I like to think that's the general trajectory). More than that, I don't think he was afraid of anything. I think he secretly liked a little excitement, even a little danger. His life had been made of it.

He certainly wasn't easily intimidated. Having been a conscientious objector during WWII and having spent time in prison as a result (and even, at one point, in solitary confinement), Albert wasn't overly concerned about what the State Department had to say. At any rate, despite my great admiration for Albert and for his and Eleanor's noble quests, I decided the time was right for me to leave. Albert and I were butting heads far too often, and probably due in some part to his advancing age, when he butted heads with me, it wasn't always calm or coherent. Nor was his wife alive anymore to act as the voice of reason. It wasn't the first time I had made up my mind to leave, but it would be the last.

Even as I walked out the door, I was fully aware that the short years I had spent working with Albert and Eleanor were unique and something I would always cherish. Their concern for others and for the environment deeply resonated with my own beliefs, and the causes these two die-hards had championed would remain dear to my heart. But now I had to leave that heady atmosphere and find a different job – and how the heck was I ever going to top that one?

The short answer is, I wasn't. At least, not right away.

In the meantime, something happened that would shatter the fabric of the community in which we lived, and forever alter many lives.

My oldest daughter, now living independently with her young son, called that April morning to alert me that there'd been some kind of shooting at Columbine High School. We lived only blocks away from the school, where all three of our girls had graduated, the last one just the year before. Our son was in junior high and due to start there the following year. Consequently, none of our children was at the school that morning as it was the one year out of the ten that we'd lived in Littleton that we didn't have a child enrolled there. Needless to say, however, many of our neighbors' and friends' children were there, including the son of one our development investors.

I was just leaving the house when my daughter called and, as we didn't yet know the extent of what was going on, we made the decision that I should go ahead and leave the house. As I listened to the car radio, I began to glean, as was everyone by now, the scope of what was taking place. I turned the car around, but was unable to get back into our neighborhood, which was now being blocked by police. I parked a fair distance away and managed to walk my way back to the house. At this point, helicopters were everywhere, as were the media and police. Things were still playing themselves out at the school and no one was sure of anything, except that the scale of this thing seemed to be unprecedented.

Not far away, my son's school was on lockdown. Ultimately, he would not be able to come home that night, spending the night with my parents instead. It was the beginning of many horrific hours, days and weeks for the community and for the world, I think – most agonizingly, needless to say, for the families of the victims.

To this day, the sound of helicopters overhead can still take me back in a very visceral way to that awful time in April. More so for my oldest daughter who worked at Swedish Hospital's emergency room where many of the victims were air-lifted, some of whom she knew.

Tragedies such as this one, especially those that cut short the lives of innocent young people (and also, in this case, a beloved teacher), shattering families in the process, have a way of putting everything into perspective for the rest of us.

Failed movies and financial worries are insignificant in the face of what is most dear.

———

I finally landed a job as the Director of a non-profit wellness center ("wellness center" has become something of a Colorado euphemism for marijuana shop, but at the time, wellness actually meant *wellness*). It was a great job, decent pay, lots of autonomy, and plenty of free massages (also acupuncture, chiropractic, etc., though I took shamefully little advantage of these). Overall, it was just the healing experience I needed. In fact, one day, while sitting at my desk under pressure to prepare for a center event, it dawned on me that no one there knew me as the woman who wore frozen peas on her head. After more than 25 years, my migraine headaches had up and disappeared!

Kim, in the meantime, continued to work in her field of expertise (well, one of them), as a Paralegal. We would both eventually find a way to finagle a four-day work week for ourselves. Apart from the fact that it's just more civilized (we should all have that prerogative!), giving ourselves one day of the week to meet and work or write was important to us, allowing us to make the money we needed to sustain ourselves, while giving us the time to keep on pursuing the dream – whatever shape that was going to take.

Then, in 2001, a lovely thing happened. After years of foot deprivation, Kim finally got a pedicure. No, seriously… she got married! (And, for that, she got a pedicure.) Remember the man who had visited the set with her sister just as things were taking a turn for the worse? The man she had little time for, whose face she could barely remember? That's the one.

From Kim:

From time to time, my sister casually mentioned her coffee buddy and co-worker (in that order), the tall, unassuming man who had visited the movie set (A Bucket of Paint) with her on an especially challenging day all those years ago. And, though I didn't give much thought to it, I enjoyed getting to know more about him through stories she'd share, especially the fact that he and I both considered the original "101 Dalmatians" one of our favorite movies! But I never realized he would resurface in my life in any way, much the less in such a significant one. I guess you never know, and that's what keeps life interesting and what hope itself is all about.

So Lynn was in my life, and in October of 2000, he and I took a trip to Southern California, joined by his sister and her husband. While planning the trip, Lynn had expressed a strong desire to go to Laguna Beach — at sunset. No other time would do. Sunset. Period. But with all the activities planned (Disneyland, Universal Studios, etc.), only a morning trip to Laguna Beach was going to work. Lynn reluctantly relented, and on the lovely morning of October 22nd, we headed out to the beach. The two of us were holding hands, strolling along the sand when, at some point, we found ourselves in a spot all by ourselves. Lynn reached out and gently took my other hand. Gazing into my eyes, he started moving in a slow, circular dance-like motion. Smiling, he asked, "Will you marry me?" It felt like the earth had stopped, yet we kept moving. So THAT's why he insisted we be on the beach at sunset! Poor guy! A morning proposal would have to do. And, though we unwittingly spoiled his perfect plan, things worked out just the same. Plus, news of our engagement was a nice surprise for his parents when he phoned his Dad that night to wish him a happy birthday!

On a beautiful day in August, Kim and Lynn were married at Denver's Botanical Gardens. After riding the emotional rollercoaster for so long, Kim was due for a hefty dose of confetti, and it was great to see it land squarely on her head.

Kim and Lynn on their wedding day

Kim and I now had something else in common besides our love of film and our *A Bucket of Paint* experience. We both had husbands with feminine first names. To this day, Lynn and Lauren continue to receive unsolicited copies of Victoria's Secret magazines through the mail. It's apparently the price they have to pay for not having masculine monikers. Some might say that's a good thing.

Time was going by and we were now living in a new millennium. But, though my parents had lived to see it, their health was on a downward spiral.

Meantime, the wellness center I managed was put up for sale. While I took the lead in negotiating the purchase of the center to my two Assistant Directors and myself, the truth was, I was not in a position to be purchasing a wellness center, regardless of the terms. I didn't have the money and, moreover, after what we'd been through with the film, I didn't want the liability. Ultimately (and pretty quickly), I stepped out of the deal. I was very fond of my incredibly capable Assistant Directors, and I think they were of me, but I doubt there were any tears shed over my decision, at least not from a business point of view — two partners, in this case, made a lot more sense than three. It had been fun and instructive and emotionally and physically nourishing at a time when I needed all of the above. But, at the end of the day, although it would mean hitting the pavement again to look for a job, I knew it was the right thing to do.

While Kim and I tried to figure out what to do next (for a long time now it seemed as if we were going in three directions at once and getting nowhere fast), I decided to take a couple of weeks to polish my existing screenplays and enter some screenwriting contests. At the top of my list was entering a screenwriting fellowship — Nicholls and Chesterfield were my two choices. It was great to have a window of time and freedom to work on my writing, and I made short order of sending off my applications. Having accomplished my immediate goal, I was on the verge of looking at job possibilities when things took a turn for the worse for my mother.

Instead of looking for a job, I ended up spending the next year taking care of my parents (living with growing dementia, my father was heavily dependent on my mother), as they slid into the finish line of an amazing and wonderful life together. Sixty-two years! (At a critical moment in the hospital, my mother would say to my father, "I want you to know that you've made my life a heaven on Earth," which pretty much summed it up.)

They'd always stayed pretty healthy, but now, as if to make up for lost time, my mother started going through the gamut of health issues – heart attack, quadruple bypass, colon cancer, stroke, pulmonary embolism, you name it. Caring for them became my life and, despite the difficulties, my singular privilege. My debt of gratitude to them is something I can never repay. They gave me life, a childhood that I'll always treasure, and the ability to laugh even through my tears.

Though Kim and I stayed in contact, we didn't spend much time together during this time. Nor could I have found the time to write, though I did keep a notepad by my bed where, at odd hours, I found myself jotting mounds of notes for a screenplay idea that just wouldn't leave my brain – a screenplay having nothing to do with pain, suffering, loss, or any of the real-life material at hand. It was, in fact, an animated feature – a story whose characters just wouldn't let me go, determined as they were to keep me smiling and looking at the bright side of things.

At some point in all of this, responses came back from my various competitions. I was a semi-finalist at both Nicholls and Chesterfield (where I was required to send three screenplays and/or a book and two screenplays) – a fair achievement, given the thousands who had applied to each. But that was where it ended. In truth, there was little room in my life at that point for anything but the task at hand, so maybe it was just as well.

Then, one day, Mom took a fall, spent nine days in a coma, and passed on from this life. Now it was time to focus on my Dad, who was completely lost without her. Ultimately, he came to live with us, and Lauren, whom my father loved (he thought there were two Laurens, which was even more special) quit his job to become his caretaker. Of course, we had no idea how long Pop would be with us. Pop didn't know much at that point, but he did know he was with those he loved and who loved him. And he never lost his sense of humor. Even in the throes of dementia, he seemed bent on keeping us laughing. His beautiful passing came three months later when he decided it was time to "go kiss his bride".

When it was all over, I felt like I'd been flattened by a steam roller. Kinda like the Road Runner, only flatter. Even *A Bucket of Paint* hadn't made such a pancake out of me. My parents had left a little money for me and my three siblings, and though the urgency wasn't immediate, I still needed to find a job. I didn't feel up to it, however – or, better put, I didn't feel there was much left of me to offer an employer. I needed time. I decided it might be wise to volunteer until such a time that I could justify my wages, so I began looking for some soul-satisfying volunteer job. In the meantime, Lauren's employer generously took him back with full and continuous benefits.

―――

Something happens to you when you put your heart and soul into a dream and fail. For one thing, as mentioned earlier, you're not too keen on taking on any more liability, financial or otherwise. From a more philosophical perspective, you realize that failure is a temporary phenomenon and is, in fact, just a part of life. To win is to keep on going. To lose is to stop trying. It's just that simple.

But the most striking thing that happens to you when you put your heart and soul into a dream and fail is that you can't ever ignore or dishonor your dreams again – not without inviting a lot of sadness and regret into your life. In short, you can't ever go back to the person you were before you put on your parachute and jumped out of that airplane. For better or worse, you've felt the air against your cheek, and you know what it feels like to fly.

How this translated for me at this point in my life, especially after *A Bucket of Paint* and after working for the likes of Albert and Eleanor, was that I was emotionally incapable of taking a job just for the money. The job would have to *mean* something to me. Obviously, need and even desperation sometimes drive us to take, and to be grateful for, whatever we can get. And, depending on our attitude and determination, whatever we can get can become a groundswell for joy and value. Whichever way the wind blew, I was determined to do my utmost to find something that I could transform into the best possible use of my time and abilities. If necessary, writing was something I could do on the side. Filmmaking, if we were lucky, we could do on the side. Maybe there was even a way to mesh all these things, to incorporate what I loved best into what I had to do. (I'd managed to do that before.) Whatever the case, I set out to find the perfect volunteer job for myself. And I found it.

―――

I sent The Survivors Center an email, asking if they needed a volunteer who spoke French, and when the answer came back in the affirmative (a lot of their clients during this period were from French-speaking parts of Africa), I interviewed with them, got the "job", and quickly set up a twenty-hours/week work schedule, job sharing with a wonderful woman – now friend – named Sarah (we not only shared a job, we shared a birthday). The Center served survivors of war trauma and torture who came to the United States fleeing the persecution of oppressive governments (deemed so by the United States). Once here, our Center (a non-profit) offered them pro bono legal assistance in obtaining asylum, as well as pro bono social, physical health, and mental health services.

It was the perfect situation for me. I was able to do volunteer interpreting for our clients and their various providers, and brush up on my rusty French in the process. Eventually, I would be offered the job of in-house French Interpreter, as well as Office Manager, and allowed that four-day work week I so much appreciated, making it possible for me to continue on my creative journey.

The most amazing part of my close to five-year affiliation with The Survivors Center was, without doubt, getting to know our clients. Their unspeakable stories, which were not only spoken, but for which I was compelled to translate, would have shaken me to the core, if not made it impossible for me to continue my job, had it not been for the amazing courage displayed by these men and women who had suffered through the worst abuses imaginable. Every day, without fail, there was a smiling face to greet me. Even where there were tears, there always seemed to be a smile on the other side. The movie-making mayhem that Kim and I had suffered was nothing in comparison to what they had had to endure.

Our clients came from all walks of life – many had been professionals – doctors, dentists, journalists, high-level government officials, successful entrepreneurs. They had lost children, parents, siblings, careers, life savings, not to mention their homeland. They had experienced war, been tortured and treated in the most painful and humiliating ways by their fellow human beings and had only barely escaped their persecutors with their lives. That they could endure the inhumanity of it all and come out the other side with a smile, still clinging to hope, still grateful for another day of life, was deeply humbling. Granted, there were a few who had tremendous difficulty surmounting their past – the young man who had lost his entire family to the horrors of war, the young girl who had had all her fingers cut off. (At the sight of this young girl, I was jolted back to

Bob's having told me that I'd want to cut off all my fingers before I would want to write again. Now, here, before me, was that metaphor's literal reality, a horribly tragic sight to behold.) I could only pray these amazing people would ultimately find the resilience to keep on going.

Once again, my life was reminding me – losing a film, in the greater context, is nothing! Bankruptcy is nothing! Another day of life is everything! Gratitude is everything!

Continuing to smile in the face of the world's horrors is a rare form of courage. But it seems to me that all smiles, regardless of circumstances, are acts of hope and courage. Smiles are defiant. Laughter is defiant. How grateful I was, and still am, for everything I experienced at The Survivors Center! Truth be told, in our own far less dramatic way, Kim and I were also survivors. And I don't think I'm too off-base to suggest that maybe, in some inescapable way, we all are.

Somewhere in all of this, I found the time to write that feature animation screenplay from the collection of notes I had made during my parents' illnesses and eventual passing. Writing it was a breeze. I was ready.

―――

In late summer of 2004, my brother Craig helped pay for Lauren and me to join him and his wife and a few friends at a villa in Tuscany. This was finally the "trip to Malta" (which, after the demise of *A Bucket of Paint*, had really become a metaphor for peace and relaxation) I had long been dreaming about.

About that time, back in Colorado, Kim was planning her own "trip to Malta" – on a very different level.

From Kim:
One morning, I woke up, turned to my husband and said, "Lynn, I'm going to film school!" While the decision may have seemed to come out of the blue, the truth

is, the idea had been quietly nagging at me for years. Lynn was not only fine with the idea, he was totally supportive. His assumption, however, was that I'd be attending film school in Colorado, which wasn't exactly how the dreamed played out in my head. I wasn't sure how we were going to pull it off, but I wanted – needed – to go to... New York, of course! So, together, we figured out a way to make things work. Instead of the traditional two or four-year stint, I enrolled in a two-month intensive program in the heart of Manhattan. Then, a week away from turning in my resignation at work, Lynn unexpectedly lost his job. I don't know which one of us cried harder, but film school would definitely have to be put on hold. Not knowing what the near future held, I contacted the school, and they agreed to hold my place (and money) until fall. Our hope was that Lynn would find another job by then, which, luckily, he did. At long last, on a sweltering day in August, the two of us made our way to the New York fifth-floor (no elevator) apartment we had secured on eclectic St. Marks Street.

Film School was made up of an international student body. In fact, there was only one other American in my class. I was also the oldest person in my section. Together, our class made sixteen short films, four of which I directed. At the conclusion of the program, my family, none of whom had ever been to the Big Apple before, flew out to New York to see the final student films and even do a little sight-seeing. It was the perfect ending to the fulfilment of a long-standing ambition, and my heart was lighter for having finally transformed that dream into reality.

Inspired by Kim's single-minded determination, I resolved to keep on plugging away at our individual and mutual objectives. I entered a few more screenwriting contests, ended up a semi-finalist in one, a finalist in another, and won the Calypso Award for Feature Screenplay for Kids at the Moondance Film Festival for that animated feature.

It wasn't long after that, that Craig was diagnosed with lung cancer, and in 2006, after a brave struggle, my dear brother passed away. Talk about smiles and laughter! Craig was defiant until the end.

Life might kill him, but he wasn't going to let it get him down. It was pretty hard to lose him though – he had become a great friend to me and my family, and a supporter as well, always interested in what I was up to, always eager to promote his sister's talents wherever he could. Shortly before he died, he said to me, "I don't think people really die as long as they're remembered, do you?" To which I'd like to respond even at this late date, *How could we possibly ever forget you?*

Craig lived in Kansas City and was the consummate sports fan. I've never met anyone who knew as much about, or who truly loved, sports as much as he did. His last words to me were a testament to this fact. Of course, he was oxygen-deprived when he uttered them, but I still think the words are pretty perfect. I had just finished telling him I loved him, knowing it would surely be the last time. He replied in that breathless, end-of-life voice – a voice I can never forget – "I love you too, Pammy. *And I love the Chiefs!*"

———

After Kim returned from film school, she put her newfound skills to work making some freelance videos, while on my end, we planned for my daughter, Courtney's, wedding. Nothing fancy – the backyard would have to do. The problem was, after years of neglect, our extremely expansive backyard was a bed of weeds – giant thistles, to be precise. In fact, I hadn't set foot in the backyard since the start of the *A Bucket of Paint* project. And now it was just too creepy. Instead, I day-dreamed about moving somewhere else, somewhere where the flowers bloomed and the butterflies, hummingbirds, and other wildlife gathered. (We did occasionally attract a fox or rabbit, or a fox chasing a rabbit – but not just any old fox, mind you – a fox that was willing to vault through a wasteland of thorny thistle to nab his prey.)

But then, one day, I reminded myself that the Buddha Land wasn't in some far-away place, but in our own creepy backyard – at least, potentially. So, in the spring of 2007, everyone – kids, spouses, etc. – put on their work pants and sun hats and made it happen. We built a patio, a flagstone path, a ground-level deck (we got some extra help with that one). We planted pots of flowers and flowering vines, a vegetable garden, and a wildflower garden with paths running through it. The word got out, and birds and butterflies began to flock there. In due course, we had a wedding there too, which Kim and Lynn attended, along with many other friends and relatives. It was beautiful. After that, I loved my backyard. I could never get enough of it. And I was reluctant to leave it when we finally did. But it taught me a lesson about potential – that it's boundless and ever-present, just waiting to be tapped even amid the worst of circumstances.

The wounds had long healed, and Kim and I now seldom spoke of *A Bucket of Paint* – mostly because it was no longer relevant to our daily lives. Sometimes we spoke of the lessons learned. Lessons we never wanted to forget. Occasionally, we allowed ourselves a moment of reminiscing, a laugh, a tear. Mostly we just continued to do what we'd always done – move forward. We might not have succeeded in making our film all those years ago, but we had triumphed in putting our lives back together and in enjoying what there is to enjoy. Moreover, we'd never given up on ourselves or on life's potential.

By now, it was becoming increasingly clear to us that the world was entering a new era of film. In fact, we were now smack dab in the middle of a digital revolution. The upshot for us – which occurred to us one fine day – was that buying a camera and making a film might actually be within our reach, investor or not, money or not. Well, okay, we might need a little money, but not stacks of it. Not millions. Not even hundreds of thousands. Surely, we could find a way to make it happen, even if we had to make it for a song. Hadn't that been the original inspiration, anyway – not the millions, but the magic?

ACT THREE

WALK-INS WELCOME — A Movie at Last!

WALK-INS WELCOME
A Movie at Last!

Summer 2007 *– For the first time since the demise of A Bucket of Paint, Kim and I find ourselves standing at the intersection of Brave and Foolhardy (well, maybe I personally revisited the corner when I jumped on that skateboard). But, looking up, we can see that the street names have changed. It's now the intersection of Now's the Time and Who Needs Millions? But even a zero budget film can't be made for zero dollars. And we're not exactly sure where we're getting the money or how much we'll need. One thing seems clear, though. The time is about as right as it's ever going to be.*

We decide to form another corporation. After some deliberation, we name it ROJée Crumbe Films, Inc. after our kindhearted and always encouraging husbands. (Lauren's middle name is Bruce; Lynn's middle name is Jerome, and if you scramble these, you'll come up with ROJée Crumbe, a fictional fellow who now has a life and identity apart from his namesakes.)

Kim and I still cherish the dream of being intimately involved with all aspects of filmmaking, but we also recognize that we'll need a great team. We'll need money for some up-front expenses too, as well as for cameras and equipment. Most of all, we'll need a lot of food.

From Kim:

Yep, here we are at that intersection again, but as Pam pointed out, the names have changed!

When A Bucket of Paint was becoming a reality, that is, when we had succeeded in raising development funds, and then when our original investor agreed to fund us, the whole thing felt surreal. Had we really put together such an incredible cast? Hey, that's our set they're building! One minute we were walking on air and the next thing you know we were staggering in slow motion — living a nightmare from which we couldn't seem to wake up.

Fast forward to buying cameras and other film equipment for our no-budget film, scouting locations, scheduling auditions for the cast and interviewing for crew positions, hearing the words, Action! and Cut! and Quiet on the set! Once again, it felt surreal. But this time it was actually… real. In a good way.

We thought out every decision and remained in control from beginning to end (at least where anything of importance was concerned). No fancy cars this time, no cappuccino-makers, just hard work and creativity and the incredible contributions of a great cast and crew. A little past experience on our part, both positive and negative, didn't hurt either.

No, this wasn't going to be A Bucket of Paint. But it was going to be a feature film. And it was going to be fun.

WHO SENT THE DOG HOME?

It was four below zero that night and everyone's body temperature was plummeting, including our dog actor, Skeeter, and his warm-hearted (but still freezing) owner, Janice. October 2009 was unseasonably cold, and prepare as we did, the multiple layers just never seemed adequate enough.

We were all gathered in (my daughter) Courtney's small backyard to film a scene of our protagonist, Claude, driving through the night. Of course, he wasn't actually driving – some distressed individual with frozen hands was rocking the car to make it seem as if the car were traveling down a bumpy road. And Pete, the actor who played Claude, was trying not to exhale, lest he should give away the arctic freeze that held even the interior of the vehicle in its grip.

Wimps that we are with regard to freezing to death, Kim and I huddled in another car parked nearby, where, by routinely scraping the windshield, we could almost keep tabs on the shoot.

the dog in question

Occasionally, we'd brave it, leave the vehicle, and try to get a more intimate sense of what was going on. But the outside world was hostile and numbing, and we quickly retreated into a car whose engine had to be turned off (*quiet on the set!*) more than it could be left on. But who was complaining? At least, we were out of reach of the wind while others had no choice but to grin and bear it.

No one had permission to enter the house, as Courtney's husband, whose work schedule demanded he be sleeping, had agreed to our coming, with the caveat that we stay out of the house. So there was no opportunity for anyone to warm up by a cozy fire or even behind a closed door. That being the case, getting the shoot over with was paramount. And brain freeze wasn't lending itself to good decision-making on anyone's part.

Jon knocked on our car window and we rolled it down just enough to make conversation possible, hoping he'd make it snappy.

"Where's Skeeter?" he asked, his lips barely able to form the words.

"Skeeter?" I replied, a little surprised at the question. "I don't know. Probably with Janice."

"Janice is gone."

Kim stepped in. "What do you mean, Janice is gone?"

"She's not here. I think they may have gone home."

However Skeeter's (*Rowdy* in the film) absence had come about (it turns out the dog had been compassionately, but prematurely, dismissed), it posed a problem, as we still needed to film him flying out the car window as a result of a car accident. This was going to be accomplished, as best we could figure, by having him jump out the window into Janice's waiting arms and somehow speeding up the film during the editing process. We'd get a number of takes, and something in there would have to work. But it certainly wasn't going to work without the dog.

It was our one and only opportunity to get the shot, as we wouldn't have access to the car again, not to mention that we had an impossibly tight schedule to adhere to. It was now or never.

Dawn put on her thinking cap. She got Courtney's permission to enter the house on tiptoe and look around for – well, she wasn't quite sure what, but something. Something that said *dog*. Something that said *Skeeter*. Something that said *Skeeter flying out of a window*. Moments later, she came out of the house, carrying a mottled-gray, but essentially Skeeter-colored, Sherpa-type of wool hat.

Jon was skeptical. We all were. But Dawn was persistent. Finally, Jon agreed to film a few takes, with Dawn lying on the car floor next to Pete at the wheel – she, surreptitiously throwing the hat out the window as Pete "crashed" the car.

No one said anything, but we were all thinking the same thing. *Nice try, but I don't think so.* We were also thinking, *Could we just get the hell out of here now and go home to our nice warm beds?* In any case, I don't think any of us expected that little trick to work.

Amazingly, it did. It not only worked. It was flawless.

But that was well into filming.

Let's back up a little.

NOT YOUR ZOMBIE FILM

We all liked Jon – a curly-haired, teddy bear of a guy – from the day he and my daughter Dawn first hooked up, and he quickly became a card-carrying member of the family. Still, it took time for us to realize that, beyond his work as a graphic designer, he had serious film aspirations and unseen, as-yet-untapped abilities. As family conversations necessarily turned to filmmaking – and the occasional vignette from the *A Bucket of Paint* saga – it became clear that Jon, who also happened to be artistically-gifted and software-savvy, might make a viable part of our filmmaking unit.

Kim, Jon, Dawn and I met at the Elephant Bar for lunch one day, cemented our arrangement, and became what we referred to from that point forward as "the team". We decided to use tax returns to purchase some nice digital cameras – one to be purchased by Dawn and Jon, and one by Kim and me. Other equipment would have to be purchased as well, and Jon did the needed research to find what we needed at prices we could afford. Ultimately, we ourselves would build a very serviceable dolly and crane. Now all we had to do was prepare a realistic budget, secure actors and crew, break down the script, and establish a shooting schedule. Oh, and a few other things.

Jon behind the camera(s)

But what script were we talking about? We quickly decided on *Walk-ins Welcome*, a no-budget pet project idea of Kim's and mine, a quirky, campy follow-up to our experience with Velvet during the development of *A Bucket of Paint*. *(What if walk-ins really did exist? And what if a walk-in had amnesia and didn't know he was a walk-in?)* There were a number of locations in the story, but we figured that here on our own home turf, we could find a way to get beyond that obstacle.

For better or worse, *Walk-ins Welcome* wasn't your typical no-budget horror story. Nor was it a zombie film. It had elements of non-terrestrial weirdness, but it wasn't typical low/no-budget sci-fi either. For lack of words to describe it, it was simply its own slightly indescribable thing. However, like many low-budget zombie, horror, and sci-fi films, it didn't take itself too seriously. In fact, it didn't take itself seriously at all. It was just supposed to be a movie in good fun

– a movie that poked fun at itself and its own subject matter. But, unlike many such films, it was also kind of sweet and romantic – what we eventually began describing as a campy, sci-fi romantic comedy. A hard sell maybe, and definitely not to everyone's taste – but, since going against the grain seemed to be our modus operandi, that wasn't our first consideration.

The material appealed to Jon in particular because he would have the opportunity to play with non-CGI (non-computer-generated) special effects. In fact, since there weren't that many special effects in the film to begin with, we revised the script (or did Jon?) to include them. Special effects can tend to escalate the budget, but we figured that, with a little creativity and a lot of tapioca (more about that later), the budget could be contained. And Jon might be able to have some fun in the process. Little did we realize how much fun we would all have.

Sherpa 1 and Sherpa 2, a.k.a. husbands, Lauren & Lynn, hamming it up between takes

THE PRICE OF AUTONOMY

Many years had passed since Kim and I had optimistically, and with naïve, bull-headed determination, set out to develop and produce a feature film from the script known as *A Bucket of Paint*.

This was not *A Bucket of Paint*.

Don't get me wrong. *Walk-ins Welcome* wasn't just silliness and good fun. It had warmth and humor too. But we had chosen it, in some sense, for the fact that it was something off the grid. We could play with it. We could take our time with it. If people didn't get it, so be it. What mattered to us was that we could make it using local cast and crew, that we wouldn't need a wheelbarrow full of money to make it happen, and that, while navigating our way through it, we would have full control over the process and be learning in earnest every step of the way. We also felt we had an obligation to ourselves, not to mention to others, to prove that we could follow through and actually make a feature film – any film!

Had money not been an object, would we have chosen some other script we had in the wings? Yes. Campy sci-fi rom-com is not representative of what I typically write, nor is it what I'm drawn to write. That being said, there was no question that *Walk-ins Welcome* was the right vehicle for what we needed to do next. From the day we met Velvet back in our *A Bucket of Paint* days, it was almost a done deal. We just didn't know it yet.

A RELATIVE PITTANCE

The first order of the day after getting our cameras and a smattering of other equipment was to shoot what we called the "pre-trailer". (The actual trailer for the film would later be made from the film footage itself.) The pre-trailer would serve three purposes: to give us some experience working as a team; to familiarize ourselves with our equipment; and to act as a vehicle for raising production money.

It would have to be made for as close to nothing as was humanly possible — which, so you won't have to google it, turns out to be about $1000 (assuming you still don't have all the equipment you need) — and some friends quickly came forward to help us out.

The front and back covers of the Walk-ins Welcome DVD

Compared to the losses incurred in the un-making of *A Bucket of Paint*, we were now talking about an investment of a relative pittance, and we felt pretty safe in thinking that no one was going to take us to court, threaten us with bodily harm, or haunt our dreams for the loss of a $250 investment. If they did, we'd just forego grocery money and pay them back. Fortunately for our stomachs, we didn't have to.

The pre-trailer wasn't anything to write home about, but in making it, we learned that, to make the film, we would have to be the epitome of organization. Kim and I are pretty organized by nature, though in vastly different ways. She keeps things neat and chronological and within reach and always has what you need when you need it, while I write all over whatever paper is available but pretty much know what I'm up to. Years ago, Kim went out and bought me lined paper, thinking the lack of real writing paper might be at the heart of my non-linear ways. This was very helpful – for about half a page. That handicap notwithstanding, I'm one of the greatest list-makers you'll ever meet (it's genetic), and I like to think that makes up for my non-anal methodology. Between us, we're generally pretty good at keeping things from slipping through the cracks. Well, except for a certain multi-million-dollar feature film. Thankfully, experience is an amazing teacher!

We also learned that, with regard to Jon's potential, we were literally sitting on a gold mine – well, no, not literally, but pretty close to it. But there was another gold mine that was equally important to the successful making of our film, and that was his life partner and Assistant Director, Dawn, who had once been a Production Assistant on the set of *A Bucket of Paint*. We jokingly called her the AD with ADHD. Nothing got by her, and while in her purview, no one slept on the job. She was more than an Assistant Director, becoming, both by default and because she rocked at it, our Production Manager. Kim and I bowed to her – not in deference, but in reverence. And then we buried ourselves in the task at hand – at least until she left the room. No doubt about it, we all worked hard, but we sometimes felt like slackers in comparison to Dawn.

So the pre-trailer was done and we put together a decent little package, but still had no idea where to turn for the money required to make the actual film. In the meantime, we were getting more practice with the cameras, shooting footage of concerts and even being asked by The Survivor Center to film that year's World Refugee Day celebration in Denver.

We were starting to feel like filmmakers. I'd like to say, *again*, but that wouldn't be quite accurate. We'd been *would-be* filmmakers before. We'd been *almost-filmmakers* before. We'd been filmmakers *stumbling over our feet* and even *falling on our faces* before. We'd been the kind of filmmakers that, in the end, must do arduous battle with life's dark forces before fighting their way back to the safety and promise of daylight. In short, now that I think of it, we were filmmakers even back then.

Though I like to look at the bright and humorous side of things as much as I can, in no way do I wish to diminish our efforts, or our filmmaking journey. Over the course of many years, beginning with *A Bucket of Paint*, Kim and I had embarked on a lot of things, created a lot of things, and accomplished a lot of things. We'd been gutsy. We had dared to try, dared to fail, and still aimed to succeed. We'd just never quite made that feature film, that's all. And now, with the pre-trailer behind us, imperfect as it was, we were ready.

THOR & ATHENA

Kim had a friend, dating back to *A Bucket of Paint* days, with whom she occasionally shared a little chit-chat and a cup of coffee. Now Kim went to him to see if anyone he knew might be interested in investing in our film. It just so happened that *he* was interested, and after a little creative bantering, we came up with a workable budget and an amount of money he and his wife were willing and able to put into it – an amount we like to tell people was well under a million dollars, which is tongue-and-cheek for $10,000. Putting this into perspective, we had raised $300,000 for just the development and interim funding of *A Bucket of Paint* and had been left with nothing to show for it. It occurred to us that, at $10,000 a pop, we could have made thirty movies from that money alone. Not union movies, but movies nonetheless. An amusing, but somewhat sobering thought. And something of a hopeful one.

Kim and I still refer to our benefactor as Thor, the Norse god of thunder, protection, and healing. To us, he's all that and more. We call his wife Athena. She's all that and more too.

Going from a once-multi-million-dollar budget to a $10,000 budget might seem like a dive from a nice, warm cliff into an ice cold ocean without any clothes on, but the fact is, we felt liberated by the financial constraints (go figure), even though we would have to be creative in ways we'd never been before, especially given the fact that some of that money was going to be spent on additional equipment. It was an exciting challenge.

LOCATION, LOCATION, LOCATION

The town of Brighton, as well as the Denver business community, were friendly and accommodating. Friends and strangers alike stepped up to help us out, providing us with vehicles, food, props, clothing, you name it. In that obliging and generous climate, we were able to secure locations without a hitch – even a bakery and beauty salon right next door to each other. But the farmhouse we needed was another story – an important consideration, since it was our protagonist's residence and factored fairly extensively into the script.

Again and again, we scouted the countryside for just the right farmhouse, but seemed to be having little luck with it. We did find one farmhouse that might have worked for our purposes, except that it was absolutely layered on the inside with dead flies. In fact, it may have been only on the double-take that we realized that the carpet was beige and not black *(eww!)*. Granted, with enough vacuum bags at our disposal, we could have sucked up all those flies, but we weren't sure where they were coming from, or why they had collectively died. Were they all on crack? Had they overdosed on poisonous fumes, or maybe even asbestos? Would we be breathing toxic air and eventually end up like them, strewn, face down, all over the carpet? We jumped in our car, threw it in gear, and sped out of the driveway, not daring to look back for fear a squadron of crack-flies might be stalking us.

About to throw up our hands and rewrite the script, we were turned onto a man who managed an expansive farm not far from Denver who was open to having us film our exterior shots there. We were informed, as a side note, that Bill Murray had shot some scenes there. Interior shots, however, would have to be filmed elsewhere, as he (not Bill Murray, but the farm manager) was not keen on having film people invade the living space of the current occupants. The verdict was disappointing, but not completely thwarting. Aside from this rather important technical glitch, the farm was perfect. We knew it wasn't going to be easy, but we were determined to find some other location to marry with this one.

And fast.

The farm we ended up using - Skeeter had to be closely watched.

Again, we scouted the countryside, as well as the city and suburbs. We tried everything, but without upping the budget (not an option), we were plumb out of luck. Finally, we sat around the kitchen table and put our heads together over a cup of tea.

Kim says she knew what I was going to say before I even opened my mouth to say it.

"We could use *our* house," I volunteered. (Good sport that he is, Lauren just smiled. Maybe he too knew what I was going to say. At any rate, if he rolled his eyes at all, the body language was internal.)

At first blush, however, this idea was about as viable as a wool hat substituting for a small dog. No one at the table warmed to it – at least, not initially. But after some thought, and true to her can-do spirit, Dawn not only came on board with the idea, but soon provided us with a detailed blueprint, matching up the farmhouse with the rooms in our house and explaining how everything could be seamlessly integrated.

There would be a few things to do, of course. Doors that would have to come down. Curtains that would have to go up. A garage door that would have to be painted forest green and a back door that would have to be changed out. Some linoleum torn up. Things like that. And we would have to beg, beg, beg the farm manager to allow us to just step foot inside the front door – just once – just enough to complete the illusion. But, in the end, Dawn assured us, if we did it right and if we crossed our fingers, we could make it work.

And work it did. Even as I re-watch the film, I'm fooled into thinking that the interiors were shot at the farm, inside the farmhouse, and not at our house. Our house wasn't quite the same after that, but then, it wasn't in the greatest shape to begin with. Before we finally sold it – it sold quickly and essentially for the asking price! – we put a lot of effort into making it shine. That *"bucket of paint"*, you know. What wonders it will do!

A LABOR OF INTEGRITY, FAMILY & FRIENDS

Soon enough, we were holding auditions – again, after all these years! The pool of local talent turned out to be extensive. Maybe as a result of certain experiences we'd had vis-a-vis *A Bucket of Paint*, it was especially important to us to build true camaraderie on the set, though, it goes without saying, you just never know how things are going to play out.

In the end, we absolutely loved our cast and crew. What a great job they all did! What joy our gayliens (gay aliens), Guy and Roger, brought to the set when we set them loose to do their thing! Impossible to remain in a funky mood around them.

Filming at our house – made sense!

But it would be presumptuous of us to say that it was a labor of love for all concerned. It wasn't. For Kim and me, however, it was both a labor of love and of integrity. Granted, we didn't sleep for an entire month, or very close to it – but who needs sleep when you're having fun?

A SAD SERENDIPITY

It's called *principal* photography for a reason, and that's because when you think you're done filming, you still have a litany of peripheral things to shoot, not to mention things to re-shoot. In any event, we set a date of Oct. 20th as the first day of a twenty-day shoot, with just a few days of filming scheduled for December. But how were we going to find the time to actually participate in the twenty days of principal photography?

Courtney cutting one of our gay alien's (gaylien's) hair. (His name is Ryan Howard.)

Fate was accommodating. Jon and Dawn were able to take time off of work. Kim's job at the time was six months on and six months off, and the October start date coincided perfectly with her off time. As for me, a not wholly-unexpected, but unhappy turn of events at The Survivors Center made it possible for me to focus exclusively on our film. In the economic downturn of the time, the Center lost its primary funding and, after a long, meaningful run, was forced to shut down.

Never have I worked for any organization where, under such trying circumstances, everyone stayed on until the last bittersweet moment, despite the knowledge that there would be no severance, nor any accrued vacation pay to fall back on. We even stuck around for the yard sale, until every piece of furniture was gone from the premises and any trace of our once-thriving haven, so beloved to so many asylum-seekers and refugees, as well to those who worked or volunteered their time there, was no longer to be seen or felt, except in our collective memories. Everyone put on a good face, but it was a tough day.

That being said, if it had to happen, the timing could not have been better for me. Taking a deep breath and drying my tears, I could plunge right into our film.

JUST ONE MORE TAKE

In the making and un-making of *A Bucket of Paint*, we had only gotten as far as rehearsals before things began to seriously unravel. Ergo, we'd never experienced the joy of shooting a feature film. It hardly needs saying that filming can be slow, tedious, redundant, frustrating, demanding and exhausting. But, for two people who craved the experience, who in the largest sense had been robbed of the experience by their own missteps — by the fetters of their karma, if you will — there wasn't a day of filming that we didn't savor.

Well, except for day thirteen. While we hadn't tried to hide the fact that a number of family members were involved (unpaid, of course), we also didn't think it was a good idea to flaunt it. Instead of calling me "Mom", for example, Dawn referred to me on the set as "Pam". It just seemed like a more professional approach, and if we had it to do over, we'd probably do it the same way. But maybe we should have put it out there more clearly from the get-go, because somewhere along the way, someone's feathers were ruffled by the "discovery" and we found ourselves laboring through a mystifyingly truculent and unruly Day 13. But, whatever it was — who knows, maybe Mercury was in retrograde — after a good night's sleep, everyone rallied and Day 14 was, in comparison to Day 13, like… well, night and day.

Filming went smoothly after that, although Jon, in his single-mindedness, drove us all nuts with his mantra of "Just one more take!" (How grateful we were during the editing process for all those takes!) Like others involved in the making of a feature film, we encountered our share of challenges, set-backs and near-calamities… having to film the wedding scenes without the bride (she was sick) and then trying to match conditions by shoveling away two feet of newly-fallen snow to shoot her end of it; bee stings; car accidents; police encounters (why is that truck driving up and down the same street with three guys huddled together in the front seat, one of them throwing up?); near-asphyxiation; minor electrocutions; the dog running away with lunch items, etc. But nothing we couldn't deal with. It was as if the gods were smiling down on us, figuring that our tenacity, at the least, should not go unrewarded.

Driving up and down our street in an endless loop…

Despite a wonderful crew, Jon still wore many hats by default, as did Dawn, Kim and I and others, which might go a long way toward explaining why we didn't sleep for a month. Kim and I cherished the opportunity to learn, both from our own duties on and off set, and from watching others in the performance of theirs. It was wonderful to finally see a feature film come together!

WRAPPING IT UP

On Dec. 13, 2009, we finally finished shooting that film we set out to make when we were young(er than we are now) and full of a wild optimism and single-minded fervor.

Not *A Bucket of Paint,* of course. And not for millions of dollars. But exactly the way we had wanted to when we first embarked on a venture to "know all there is to know". This time, we had taken a real hands-on approach, learning every nuance of the process on what was essentially a zero budget.

at the wrap dinner party

The wrap party was a blast. Not because it was expensive (it wasn't) or wild and crazy (it wasn't), but simply because we could rest easy and smile, knowing we had finally done it. Of course, post-production still lay ahead and would go on for months, stretching into years. In fact, it never seemed to end. In fact, we never *thought* it would end. So, even though we had finally done it, the fact is we weren't actually (not by a long-shot) ... done.

BACK BY POPULAR REQUEST – A PING-PONG TABLE!

Did I mention that Jon loves playing with special effects, and that if I ever hear the word "tapioca" (the mainstay of our home-made special effects formulas) again, I might have to go running down the street screaming? Countless evenings were spent in our kitchen, i.e., our laboratory, experimenting with various tapioca concoctions until we had virtually tried anything and everything one could ever attempt (barring only a few unmentionable things) with that starchy substance. This much is for sure. Knowing what I now know about its other-worldly elasticity and general ability to mutate into eerie creations, and despite its purported nutritional goodness, never again will I eat a bowl of tapioca pudding, hot or cold. For her part, Kim gags at only the sound of the word.

Despite our general distaste for tapioca, we bestowed a screen credit on our makeshift special effects laboratory, Picatoa Labs (another word scramble, we apparently never tire of them), in honor of our gooey nemesis.

Due to time constraints (Jon had to make a living), money constraints (there wasn't any left), and a big learning curve (among a thousand other glitches, we'd have to ADR, or re-record the audio, for all the bakery scenes), post-production took nearly four years to complete. One of the highlights of the post-production phase was being affiliated with Jason Schimmel, one of the few non-Colorado residents involved with the making of our film, who wrote the score for us. We were thrilled with the outcome, as well as with the contributions of other incredibly talented musicians like Carla Kihlstedt (who did vocals for the opening credits), as well as Chris Sauthoff (Citrus) and the members of the Tumbleskunks, a band formed specifically for the film, made up of a group of talented Denver musicians.

One of Kim's and my favorite projects was staging the backdrop for the opening credits. Jon's vision was to set up a layered display of myriad items related to the film, to the main character, and to the passing of the seasons on the farm – a veritable tableau of life – on a ping-pong table in our basement. Yay – a ping-pong table again! But this time the vibes would be different. The opening credits turned out to be a favorite part of the film, both musically and visually.

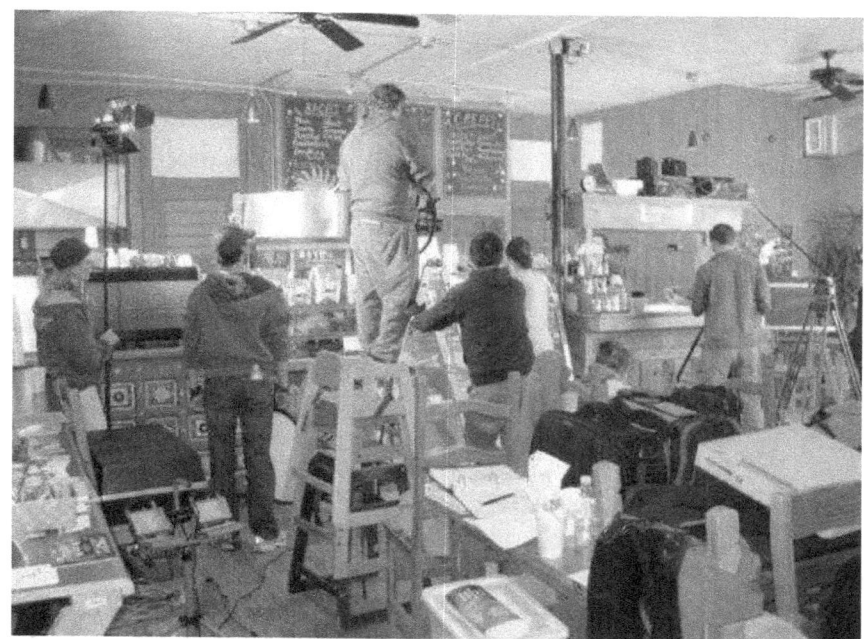

Filming at the bakery, despite a noisy cooler...

Finally, after the coming and going of innumerable deadlines, we called our movie "done". The team – Kim and I, Jon and Dawn – and sherpas Lauren and Lynn, went out to dinner to celebrate, toasted heartily to our accomplishment, and fell face-first into our plates. Well, not quite, but almost.

MISTAKES, WE'VE MADE A FEW

There's no denying we made mistakes along the way in the making of *A Bucket of Paint*, culminating in the fact that we never got it made! But the truth is, all fiascos aside, no film set or film production is free of problems, mistakes, personal conflict, and occasional ire. That's life and, as the saying goes, that's entertainment. And, no matter how hard you try, there will still be some people who plain old don't like you just because… well, just because you're you, and also just because they're who they are. That being said, Kim and I felt pretty fortunate to have worked with such a wonderful group of people. It was our resolve, as well as Jon's and Dawn's, to make *Walk-ins Welcome* the best possible experience for everyone. In great part, this earnestness was returned, and conflict and ire were kept at a happy minimum.

Even so, there were a few bumps in the road. For example, though we didn't freely and immediately distribute the *Walk-ins Welcome* DVD to everyone who worked on the film (there was no money left in the coffers), we eventually did the only thing you can when you realize you've made a mistake – cringe and do your best to rectify it.

Then there was the title of the film itself – *Walk-ins Welcome*. Try putting that on the marquis and see how many people think they can just walk in for the show, i.e., see how many "walk-ins" you actually attract (which, from another perspective, could be a good thing). But on DVD, or streamed, void of the possibility of actual walk-ins, that little problem is no longer a problem, just something to laugh about in hindsight. In spite of that little hitch, we have to say we still love the title and wouldn't go back and change it even if we could.

Dawn and Jon in front of a film festival venue

You wouldn't be human if you didn't make mistakes – in fact, if you're not making mistakes, you're probably not doing anything (or anything to rock the boat). Either that, or you're a walk-in.

SUFFER WHAT THERE IS TO SUFFER

Spring of 2013 came with some tough moments. I was hospitalized for a short while with a serious health issue, then released, only to hear a few days later that my youngest brother, Johnny, had suddenly and unexpectedly passed away. It was too hard to grasp – my little brother, so full of life and laughter! That night, I made myself watch a movie (a comedy) in his honor (it's what he would have wanted), and I told myself that if I lived through that night, I would live to be 102.

ENJOY WHAT THERE IS TO ENJOY

That summer, at the Intendence Film Festival, in Kim's hometown and on my birthday, our wacky *Walk-ins Welcome* won both the *Audience Favorite* and *Best Feature* awards. Our friends, family and other film-goers lined up around the block to see our film, and the festival granted us another showing to accommodate our appreciative crowd.

Soon thereafter, our film premiered at the Oriental Theater, a historic Denver venue dating back to the 1920s. People filled the seats and had a great time. All in all, it was an unforgettable experience and, in no small way, a dream come true. Even the question and answer session that followed on stage felt tantamount to scaling the summit of a hitherto unconquerable peak where our voices could now be heard for miles (well, okay, maybe half a block).

THE MOST IMPORTANT ATTRIBUTE

My mother used to say, "All children should be raised by poverty-stricken parents." Well, I'm not sure that's an absolute, but I get her point, which (I believe) was this: the most important human attribute may just be a sense of appreciation, which money and good circumstances alone do not guarantee, and which the challenges of hardship can serve to foster.

There is no doubt that Kim and I are stronger and more appreciative of life for the difficulties we experienced as a result of the downfall of *A Bucket of Paint*. Losing the farm was tough, but the lessons we learned and embraced in the process continue to serve us well.

As for Lauren and I, the glue that keeps us together is still holding strong – maybe all the more so for what we've weathered together. And, despite the financial and emotional turmoil we endured at a critical time in our children's upbringing, our kids have all grown up to be kindhearted, appreciative and contributive adults whose beautiful spirits never fail to inspire us.

Pam (left) and Kim in 2013, after the making of Walk-ins Welcome, twenty years after they first set out to make A Bucket of Paint

Life, so far, has been an adventure – sometimes a walk in the sun, sometimes a walk in the rain without an umbrella – but an adventure all the same and one we wouldn't trade for anyone else's.

My parents, my brothers, Craig and Johnny --- Kim's Dad and her brother, Tommy – they're all with us every day, rooting us on. Our joy is their joy, our victories theirs. We face every day with gratitude in our hearts for the new beginning that greets us every morning.

―――

Sometimes we like to imagine that, in some parallel universe, things went right for *A Bucket of Paint*. The Producers didn't blow it, or maybe Miramax rescued it, and it's now in reruns on TCM, prefaced by a word or two of praise and adulation from Robert Osborne and the co-host of the day – just for the heck of it, let's say Oprah.

But then, we think, no… this is the Universe we live in, this is our life, these are our lessons, and as I whispered in my father's ear as he gently passed from this world:

"It's all good."

Today, Kim and I have joined the many independent filmmakers out there who forge ahead with or without major investors, then do their best to make their films available to as wide an audience as possible.

That done, never forgetting the lessons of the past, we continue to hold our heads up high, put one foot in front of the other (and sometimes in our mouths), and keep on going, with the spirit that never giving up is, in itself, the greatest victory.

AFTERWORD

Parakeets Unfrozen

One day, my granddaughter, Josephine, was bicycling through the park with her father and brother when a parakeet landed on her head. They named him Thunder (after the stormy weather that afternoon) and took him home.

Not long before, Josephine's father had had to put down a young bird who, despite his parents' valiant attempts at protecting him, had been severely injured by a crow. They'd gone on that bike ride to lift their spirits, and Thunder had mystically obliged.

Though Thunder was a willing captive, it was clear he was lonely for some same-species company. Enter Lightning, store-bought and not quite as friendly a guy, but loveable just the same. I always enjoyed hearing Thunder and Lightning chit-chat with each other, undoubtedly sharing their observations on the foibles of humanity, or watching them take off from home-base (their large cage) to land on foreign soil (the top of someone's head).

So when my daughter asked us if we would keep the birds at our house, as they had become too noisy during the day for her husband to sleep, we said yes without hesitation. Anyway, I love birds. I owned a cockatiel once and considered him a friend without parallel. I even eulogized him with a poem after he died. However, I made the cardinal (no bird pun intended) mistake of sharing the poem with my class, only to be blown off the stage by my classmates' unsuppressed laughter. I was mortified. Mostly, I realized at a young age that when the world stops for you, it doesn't necessarily stop for anyone else.

Anyway, Thunder and Lightning came to stay, and thrived for a while – until we had a kitchen counter put in and were told that the glue was especially toxic to birds, at which point my daughter quickly, but temporarily, retrieved them. Thunder spent the next day snuggled against her neck, unwilling to leave her for a moment. That night he passed away, which saddened all of us, and yet, there was something lovely about his choosing the manner and timing of his death. She brought him (and Lightning) back over, along with some miniature roses for Thunder's burial bed, and we all held a ceremony in the backyard, expressing gratitude for his presence in our lives.

So now it was down to Lightning. I admit that I didn't appreciate the way he had sometimes bullied Thunder or always had to be first in line for the spinach leaf. But I made up my mind to befriend him, recognizing that he must be feeling lonely without his second-fiddle buddy around. Every day, I shared my thoughts with him and nudged my way closer to his heart. Initially reluctant to fly around the room solo, he eventually became comfortable with the idea, squeezing his way out of the cage and flying into the kitchen to perch on a chair to watch the goings-on. To my satisfaction, we were becoming true friends.

One morning in June, Lauren and I headed out the door to attend a meeting – a twentieth anniversary celebration of a Buddhist event in Denver. The year 2016 was also an anniversary year for Kim and me – twenty years since the demise of *A Bucket of Paint*.

In the spirit of flap-happy parakeets, time flies by with barely a woosh.

"See you later, Lightning Blue Sky Sweetie Pie (now that we were buddies, that was my super-corny, but official, name for him)!" I said as we left the house.

On the way home from the high-spirited event, I received a text from my oldest daughter (and original owner of the birds), suggesting that it was more important than ever that we participate in the Pride Fest parade taking place the next weekend in Denver, given the tragic happenings in Orlando, Florida. Hearing the terrible facts (I hadn't heard them yet), my spirits took a dive. But I agreed. In whatever small way we could, we needed to stand up and infuse the planet with the depth of our support and humanity.

As we entered the house, our daughter Courtney, who had just arrived, greeted us with, "I found some feathers on the couch, and I can't find Lightning." My eyes fell level to the furniture, where a few tiny tufts of downy feathers barely blemished the couch.

I knew in a flash that the dog had eaten him.

In one single, life-effacing bite.

Elvis is a big dog.

With innocent eyes.

Who doesn't like any manner of flapping.

As the search party took the couch apart and rifled through every nook and cranny of the upstairs, I sobbed and cried aloud with a single, cryptic refrain. "It's not fair! It's not fair!"

Later, I would wonder what I meant by that. *What* wasn't fair? Life? Dogs? Despicable humans?

As for Elvis, I instantly forgave him, as did my daughter – with the caveat that he can be an asshole sometimes. But the dog wasn't at fault. Given the bird's new penchant for leaving the cage on a lark (no bird pun intended), the human should have made sure the dog wasn't sharing living space with the bird.

Small retribution, but Elvis did throw up, though nothing bird-related. Later (not right away), we were able to joke that he'd been feeling a little "under the feather".

We buried those tiny tufts next to Thunder and planted some multi-colored flowers at the site. My daughter reclaimed her cage.

As the days went by, I shared the story with Kim, while earnestly searching for the symbolism. Native Americans have long viewed birds as symbols of freedom and light-heartedness. Makes sense, doesn't it? Birds soar above it all, where we sometimes wish we could be, looking down on our troubles from the greater perspective. At the spreading of my brother Johnny's ashes, a bird flew down to a low-hanging branch and regaled a whole group of us with his unrelenting song, to the point where we all agreed the event was undeniably otherwordly. Clearly, the message was not to worry – Johnny's soul was soaring free.

But symbolism is blessedly flexible. It can be anything you want it to be.

And yet, what symbolism could Kim and I possibly assign to Lightning's having disappeared in one mouthful, that would be – for lack of better words – palatable to us?

"But, Pam, that's it!" exclaimed my friend Kelly over a bowl of pad thai. The day you and Kim left the studio – the day your film went down – didn't you call that *the day of the frozen parakeets*?" And now, she pointed out, twenty years later, the parakeets, which had been in a deep-freeze for so long, were back. Back to tell us in no uncertain terms that we were free. Our karma – that particular aspect of it – was gone.

In a single mouthful.

Barely a feather left behind.

Poof!

Or maybe, *Woosh!*

It's a nice thought, albeit one which some might find a little hard to swallow (bird pun intended). Still, I got goose (here we go again) bumps when the words came out of her mouth.

And what the hell. Kim and I are flexible enough to believe it.

Parakeets unfrozen. End of story.

www.ingramcontent.com/pod-product-compliance
Lightning Source LLC
Chambersburg PA
CBHW051648040426
42446CB00009B/1030